Darryl Bartlett

WordPress

In easy steps is an imprint of In Easy Steps Limited
16 Hamilton Terrace · Holly Walk · Leamington Spa
Warwickshire · United Kingdom · CV32 4LY
www.ineasysteps.com

In Easy Steps Limited supports The Forest Stewardship Council (FSC), the leading international forest certification organisation. All our titles that are printed on Greenpeace approved FSC certified paper carry the FSC logo.

Printed and bound in the United Kingdom

ISBN 978-1-84078-634-7

Contents

1 Introduction to WordPress

This chapter introduces you to WordPress and some of the things you can build with it. You will also be guided through installation and planning.

Overview

There are quite a lot of people out there who think WordPress is just a blogging platform. This is far from the truth! WordPress can build the simplest blog all the way up to a professional, complex website – there really are no limits! WordPress is a powerful tool, which now accounts for 22% of all websites on the Internet (at the time of writing).

WordPress is becoming a great starter point for new web designers and developers, since it's a great starter point to get your website online, and it's fairly simple to pick up. As new developers become more comfortable with the platform, they can then extend their own skills to advance their own websites.

A lot of professional web developers are turning to WordPress to build sites for clients as it's a powerful tool, it cuts development time, and it provides a great content management system (CMS) so that their clients can add content themselves.

Bloggers are finding it a great platform to work with, as they can add content quickly and easily without having to have a lot of technical knowledge.

This book will provide you with all the basic fundamentals needed to help you on the road to building your website or blog with WordPress. It doesn't matter if you're new to the whole concept of web development or blogging, as the book will guide you through each step with screenshots and detailed text to help you progress through each chapter. If you are a professional web developer, there will be things in the book that can help boost your knowledge of WordPress and how it works. You can then bring this knowledge to your own projects.

What will I need?

For this book you are going to need two things.

- **A domain name:** (For example: **www.hello.com**).
- **Web Hosting:** This is space online that you use to host your website. You pay a monthly or annual fee to rent space online. For the purpose of installing WordPress, I will be using a host called HostGator.

Now you are ready, it's time to get started!

Why Use WordPress?

Web Development was once considered a gigantic task involving hardcore programming skills. Websites were developed using text editors as simple as note pads. However, with advancements in web development technologies, people with little or absolutely no programming experience also began to find their feet in this arena. This happened owing to the development of content management systems such as WordPress, Joomla, Moodle and similar web development platforms. These content management systems allow layman users to develop professional looking websites. Choosing a content management system depends on various factors. However, we will focus on why WordPress CMS is an excellent choice for developing websites.

Based on Open-Sourced Technologies

WordPress is an open source CMS and can be tweaked and edited by anyone to fit their needs. WordPress is based on PHP which is an open sourced server-side programming language. WordPress uses MySQL database for data persistence and storing content such as posts, comments and images etc. MySQL is also open source and freely available.

Easy to Install and Manage

Installing WordPress is an extremely simple task and requires few clicks of the mouse. Most of the domain hosting companies, such as HostGator and GoDaddy, provide one-click installation services for WordPress. Usability of WordPress is not limited to installation; once installed, it is also very easy to manage via WordPress dashboard. For instance, creating menus, pages, posts, adding images and setting titles is a matter of few clicks and entails no programming skills.

Styling using Themes

There are thousands of WordPress themes freely available. These themes can be used to define an overall style for your website. Themes can be tweaked to achieve desired styling functionalities. There are also premium themes out there for a small cost, so no two websites will ever look the same. Themes are a great way for early developers to learn how websites are built and it takes out the technical challenge so you can work on the content and look of the website, without having to worry. For the advanced designer, you are able to use the editor to tweak your themes even further, or even create your own.

...cont'd

Enhanced Functionality Via Plugins

WordPress websites can be enhanced easily via several "plugins". WordPress themes, by default, come with basic functionalities. However, additional functionalities can be added via plugins. For instance, if you want to add a login widget to your website, you can use login plugins. Similarly, in order to add a contact form on your website, a contact form plugin can be used, not just to add the form to your page, but also to store and send on any queries that come through your website. There are many freely available plugins that can be used to enhance functionality of a WordPress website.

Great Support via Large Development Community

WordPress has one of the largest software developer communities. The immense developer support allows users to solve their WordPress issues immediately. Also, owing to the large developer community, rapid updates and patches are developed which solve issues that arise in any theme or plugin etc. Additionally, if you ever come across any problems, then you can always post in the support forum and be sure to get a quick response to your problem:

http://WordPress.org/support/

SEO (Search Engine Optimization) Friendly

WordPress websites are extremely SEO friendly. Companies spend thousands of dollars to rank their websites high on Google page ranks. The good thing about WordPress is that Google, for some reason, rates WordPress websites higher owing to its built-in SEO features. There are also a number of really good SEO plugins out there to help guide you through the process of SEO and help your website rank better with the search engines.

Conclusion

Though there are many CMSs currently available in the market, WordPress is the best place to start, it is extremely easy to learn, flexible to tweak, open-sourced and SEO friendly. Also, with a large developer community, you are likely to get instant help and support for any issue that arises during your website development endeavours.

What Can I Build?

As previously mentioned, WordPress is not just a blogging platform. You can build a number of different websites using WordPress. Here are just a few things you can build when you get more familiar with the platform.

- **E-Commerce Website:** Have you ever wanted to have your own online shop? A website that can accept payments? Well you can do just that with WordPress. There are a number of different plugins you can use, one of which is free is WooCommerce (see Chapter Six).
- **Business Website:** You will be surprised just how many business websites are made using WordPress. You can build a very professional website without having to know any technical languages.
- **Online Forums:** You might think that Forums are extremely difficult to create, but WordPress can make it a lot easier. There are plugins out there to help you create your own message board, so you can build a community in no time (see pages 123-128).
- **Portfolio:** If you are an artist or a photographer, then you might want to build a site to showcase your skills. With WordPress you can do just that, as there are a number of pre-made templates out there to help you show off your talents.
- **Membership Website:** If you are looking to build a site with various membership levels, for example a site with free and premium content, then you can do just that. Yet again, there are some good plugins out there to help you, and you can create numerous levels of membership (see pages 135-140).
- **Responsive Website:** There are plenty of templates out there that will optimize your website across a number of different mobile and tablet devices, so you will never have to worry how your website looks on different platforms.
- **Directory/Listings Website:** Maybe you are thinking of starting a job site? Or a classified ads site? Well you can with WordPress!

The list goes on! This is just a taster of what you can do.

WordPress Hosting

Hosting WordPress through an external host is probably the best way to get your site off the ground, as there are no restrictions and it is the least expensive option.

To install WordPress you are going to need some space online. I recommend a company called HostGator (**www.hostgator.com**). It is very well priced, offers 24 hour support and is very simple to set up WordPress on. There are various hosting companies out there that provide one-click installs for WordPress these days, which is great for new developers and bloggers. You can choose to set up your site using WordPress.com. However, there are some restrictions (see page 15).

Setup a HostGator Account

To get started, sign up for a HostGator account at **www. hostgator.com** and if you don't already have one, pick a domain for your site. You can do both on HostGator. This is the first step to getting your WordPress site on the road!

When you sign up you will be sent an email with your Control Panel login – something like the one shown below.

Plan: Shared
Control Panel Address: https://controlpaneladdress.hostgator.com
Username: yourusername
Password: yourpassword

Navigate to the control panel address in your web browser, and enter your username and password to log in to the control panel. You should be presented with something like this:

2 Scroll down the Software/Services section and click on **Quick Install**

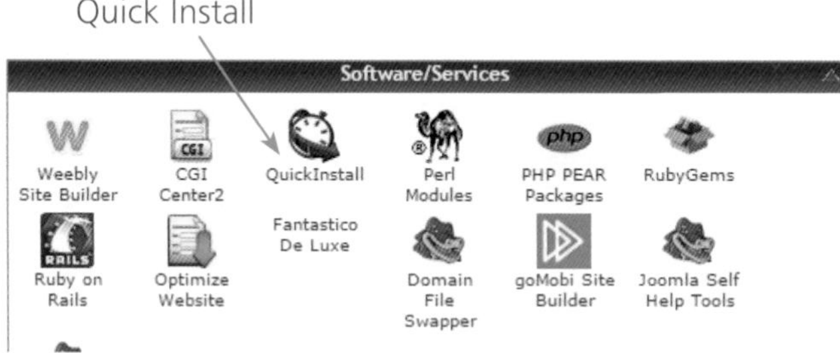

3 Next, find **WordPress** under the Blog Software section

4 Click **Continue** inside the WordPress box - you should now be presented with this form

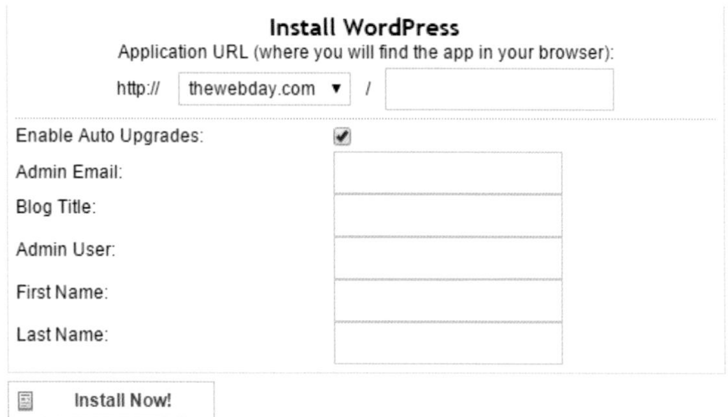

5 Fill out the form; here are some pointers:

If your domain name was *http://www.biscuits.com* and you wanted your website to show up under that address then you would leave the Application URL field blank. However, if you wanted it to load under a sub-domain, like *http://biscuits.com/digestives*, then you would type "digestives" in the Application URL field.

Application URL: You should leave this blank as this will install WordPress on your main domain.
Email: Enter the email address you wish to use for admin. Your password will be emailed to this address.
App version: Leave this as it is, unless you want another version installed.
Blog Title: This is what you want to call your blog or website.
First Name: Your first name goes here.
Last Name: Your last name will go here.

6. Once you have filled out the fields, click the **Install Now** button. You should now get a message saying your installation is ready

Congratulations!
Your installation is ready. You can access it now by going here. If there is any login information, it will have been sent to the email address you provided.
Admin Area: http://thewebday.com/wp-admin
Username:
Password:

7. You can now access WordPress by going to **http://www.yourdomain.com/wp-admin**

Remember to replace *yourdomain* with the domain you registered. You will now be presented with your WordPress login screen.

This page is where you or any other members of your website will always log in. You can tick the **Remember Me** box so that the website automatically logs you in.

Keep your login details in a safe place.

You can reset your password at the login screen. Click the **Lost your password?** button link at the bottom of the login panel.

It can take up to 24 hours for your domain to become active once registered with HostGator, so don't panic if you can't access the admin panel straight away.

Using WordPress.com

If you don't want to go through the WordPress installation stages with an external host, then you can use WordPress.com to host your site. You can host a free site with limitations or pay a yearly fee to lift the limitations. There are currently three plans in place.

- **Free: $0 a year**
- **Premium: $99 a year**
- **Business: $299 a year**

The free package does hold quite a lot of limitations. Firstly, you can't use your own custom domain and you can't customize the design. You will also pay to remove the ads. You can pick one of the WordPress domains. For example, if you were building a site on table tennis, you might choose **tabletennis.WordPress.com**

There are more limitations to using WordPress.com than with an external host like HostGator.

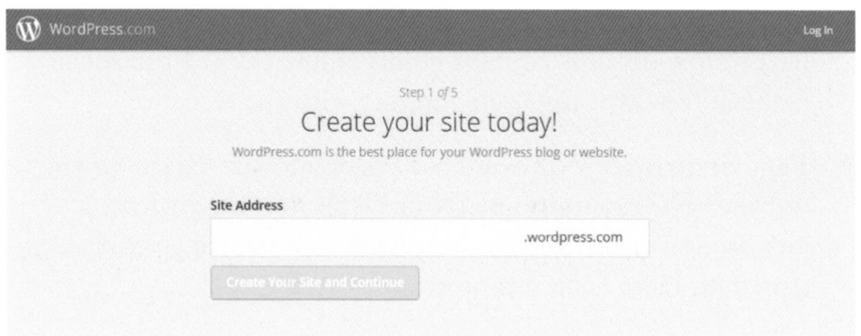

FTP stands for File Transfer Protocol. An FTP client is a piece of downloadable software that allows you to easily move files from your computer to a web host or another computer (see page 163).

The package you choose depends what functionality you need from your site. It can work out cheaper to use an external host and there are no limitations. However, it is much easier to set up using WordPress.com and your website is ready to go straight away. Bear in mind that you can only use WordPress.com themes and you can't use custom plugins or have FTP access to your files.

The setup on WordPress.com is very simple. You will be walked through a number of steps to set up your new blog/website.

Once set up, you will be able to log-in in the same manner as you would if your site was self-hosted by going to:
http://www.yourdomain.com/wp-admin

Planning Your Website

Planning is a key part of any project. You need to cover everything, all the way from design through to implementation.

Now we have gone through the installation stages, before we get our hands dirty with the interface, we are going to have a look at the important process of planning a WordPress website.

- **Research:** The area you should start with is research. Have a look at websites similar to what you want to build. For example, if you are building a technology blog, you may want to look at other technology blogs. Compare the successful and unsuccessful ones. What are the successful ones doing better? What content is engaging to the readers? How are the owners interacting with their customers? DO NOT copy other websites – this is key and will get you nowhere. You need to make sure your content is unique. Research is a valuable way to build a more successful site.
- **Brainstorming:** Now it's time to sit down with a cup of coffee and a notebook and start brainstorming your website, what is going to go on there, what pages are you going to have? How often is content going online? Will I use social media? How will my users interact with the website?
- **Page Structure:** Will you have pages and sub-pages on your website? For example, an About Us section might have a jobs section as a sub page. You need to organize your page structure. Here is an example:

  - **Home**
  - **About Us**
    - Jobs
    - Our Office
    - History
  - **Services**
    - Web Design
    - Graphic Design
    - Web Hosting
    - Printing
  - **Events**
    - This Year
  - **Blog**
  - **Contact Us**

- **Plugins:** If you are looking to add functionality to your website, you may need to research which plugins you will need and find out what the best ones are. There are plenty of free plugins out there but if you are going to spend any money on them, then you need to know what you are buying first (see Chapter 5).
- **Project Management:** Do you have milestones or deadlines in mind? Make sure you keep a schedule, and stick to it. If you want to meet your goals you need to keep a tight schedule. It's the key to a successful website.
- **Web Hosting:** Who am I going to host my website with? How much is it going to cost me? How reliable are the hosts? These are all important parts of planning your website.
- **Domain Name:** A domain is a very important part of building a website; you want to have a catchy name. Don't make your domain too long; you want people to remember it. You can always point other domains at your website as well, which is another thing to bear in mind. Domain pointing allows you to direct multiple domains to the same website.
- **Website Backups:** Make sure you are keeping backups of your site; daily would be ideal but if not then every other day. You never know if the web server is going to go down or get hacked. You will sleep easier at night knowing you have a backup (see pages 175-178).
- **Payment Methods:** If you are building a web shop, then you should think about what payment methods you want to offer. PayPal is probably the best and easiest one to set up and most people are using it these days.
- **Social Media:** Whatever website you are building, social media is a very important part of growing your audience. Be sure to share your content through as many social media channels as you can. Twitter, Facebook, YouTube and LinkedIn are the main ones.

This may seem like a long list, but it is important to keep each step in mind so that your web development will go smoothly.

Blog vs Website

Sometimes there is a lot of confusion when it comes to WordPress. Some people ask things like:

- Does my WordPress site have to look like a blog?
- Does my WordPress website have to have a blog?

Let's clear this up before we start.

WordPress Blog

Below is a screenshot of a blog built with WordPress. You will notice that the homepage lists a number of blog posts created by the user. Now, this may be fine with you, especially if you are building a blog about yourself, but what if you are building a website for your business?

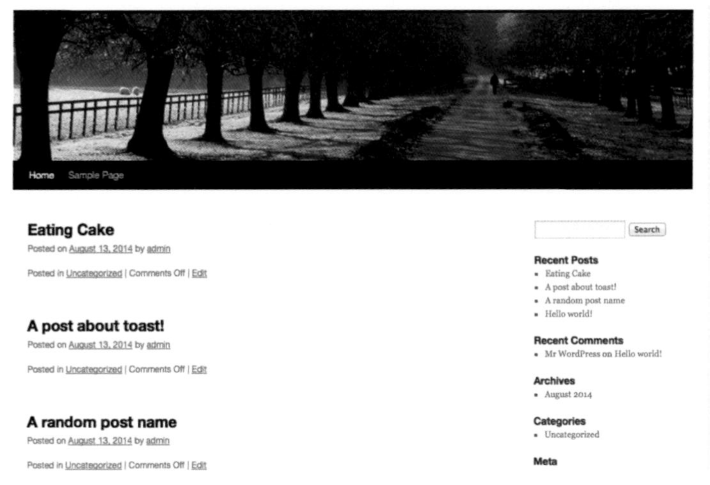

Example Blog

WordPress Website

You can easily specify a different page to become your homepage, if you don't want your website set out like a blog. You don't even have to have a blog on your website if you don't want to. However, you can still have a company blog set up but as a different page altogether. A business is likely to have their services outlined on the homepage.

Business Site Menu

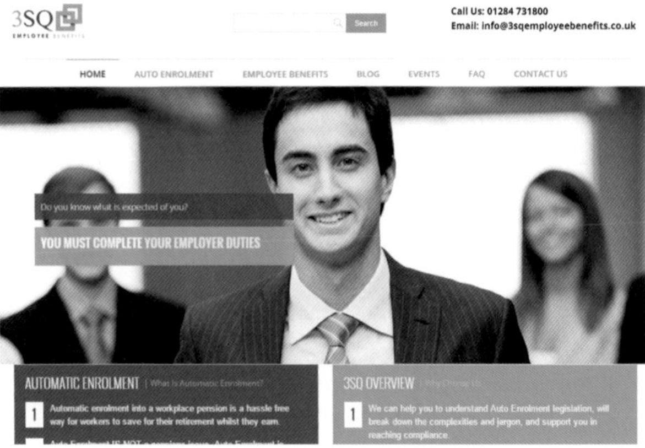

Example Business Website

Most companies or start-ups will have a blog these days, even if it's not their front page. It's a good way of interacting with their customers and it gives them something to share via social media.

Website

- Content is mainly static apart from a blog or forum section
- More of a digital storefront eCommerce
- Professional look
- Much more functionality
- Pages about products and services

Also, remember that with a website, sometimes the only way for your customers to communicate with you is through the contact form.

Blog

- Content is updated more frequently
- Newest content appears near the top
- Usually arranged by category or date
- Google loves blogs because the content is fresh
- Not formal
- Users can interact via a commenting system

The last thing to bear in mind is that a blog is still a kind of website. Most people used to choose to set up a blog because they lacked the programming skills to create a website, but now WordPress makes anything possible!

Business Websites

The Internet has revolutionized the world – it has become a global village and now everyone is linked by just a few mouse clicks. Businesses are taking advantage of huge customer presence on the Internet. Presently, 99% of successful businesses and industries have Internet presence either via social media networks or dedicated websites. There are several reasons for having a dedicated website for a business.

Huge Number of Potential Customers

The Internet user population is in the billions and many of these users search a product on the Internet before purchasing it. They compare the products offered by different companies and then make a decision about what to buy.

Cost Effective Marketing Tool

Websites are one of the cheapest marketing tools ever invented. A website can cost as little as $10-20 to start. All you need to do to set up a live website is to buy a domain and hosting and with little knowledge of any of the CMSs, you can create your very own website.

Easy Customer Interaction

Websites allow businesses to rapidly interact with their customers. Most websites now contain a "contact us" form where users can leave comments and queries whenever they want. Also, websites are live 24/7; therefore, potential customers can get information about products or services irrespective of the time-zones.

Global Presence

A company cannot open outlets in every corner of the world unless it generates billions of dollars of revenue, which is not the case with every company. The best possible way to have a global presence and reach potential customers located at diverse geographical locations is to have an international website.

Good First Impression

Companies and businesses with an official and registered website are considered more authentic and garner better customer trust, compared with businesses that do not have a website. A visually pleasing and easy to navigate website creates a good first impression and can be used to convince customers to stay on the website for longer periods of time, eventually resulting in business.

2 Dashboard & Users

This chapter introduces you to the WordPress Dashboard and how to find your way around. You will also be introduced to the Users section.

Dashboard Overview

We will be using WordPress version 4.0 throughout this book.

The WordPress dashboard is the control panel of your WordPress website. You can control every component of your WordPress website via this dashboard. You can change the theme of your site, manipulate various visible areas of your site and change the behavior of posts and comments underneath the posts. You can also add users to your website through the dashboard and can also assign different roles to those users.

This section presents a brief overview of various menu items on your dashboard along with their functionalities. We will not dig deeper into the nitty-gritty of each menu item. However, after reading this chapter, you will be aware of what each individual item on the dashboard does and what functionality can be achieved through the item. So, let's jump straight to work!

Admin Bar

Once you log in to the dashboard of your website, you will see lots of menus and messages in different windows of your dashboard. Don't worry about them; we will explain everything.

After you log in, you should see page similar to the screenshot below:

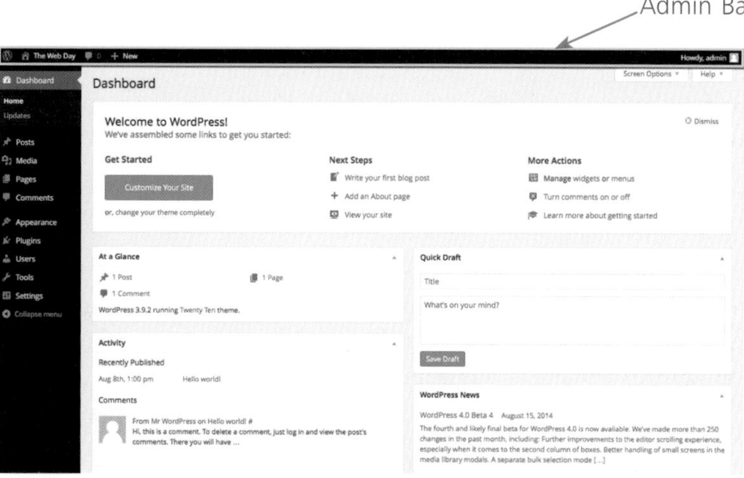

In the screenshot, at the top of the page, you should see some menu items (highlighted by a yellow rectangle). Collectively, these menu items are called the toolbar. Let us briefly discuss each of these menu items one by one, starting from the left.

Admin Bar Links

Wordpress.org is a great place to find plugins, resources, support, forums, and you can even download WordPress files from here. It is mainly for those who have used an external host for their WordPress set up.

WordPress Icon

Hovering your mouse over this icon opens a dropdown menu which contains links to WordPress resources such as WordPress.org, documentation resources and feedback etc. If you want to have a look at documentation, or you want to leave feedback etc. you can use these links.

Visit Site

Displays the title of your website. A small house icon is also displayed to the left of this item. If you click this item, you will be taken to the homepage of your website while logged in as an authorized user. If you hover your mouse over this icon, a dropdown list with one link appears which shows **Visit Site**.

Plugin Update

This will only appear if you have plugins that need updating. It will usually display a number next to it, telling you how many plugins need updating. Clicking this link will take you through to a page where you can update the plugins.

Comment Moderation

The fourth item from the left on the toolbar is the comment moderation menu. If you have specified that every post or comment needs to be moderated before publication, all the comments awaiting moderation can be moderated from here.

New Item

The last item on the toolbar on the left side is the **New** item. This item contains links to pages where a new Post, Media, Page and Link etc. can be created. If you hover your mouse over this item, you will see these options appear.

Admin Panel

Howdy, admin

If you look at the top right of the window, a link named "Howdy Admin" is displayed. This link contains the information about the logged in user. If you have assigned a different name to the admin, this link would display a different name. Basically, through this link, you can edit your admin profile. You can also choose to log out from here by selecting **Log Out** from the dropdown.

Dashboard Menu Options

We have briefly explained all the menus on the top toolbar. Now let's look at the menu options on the left hand side of the dashboard.

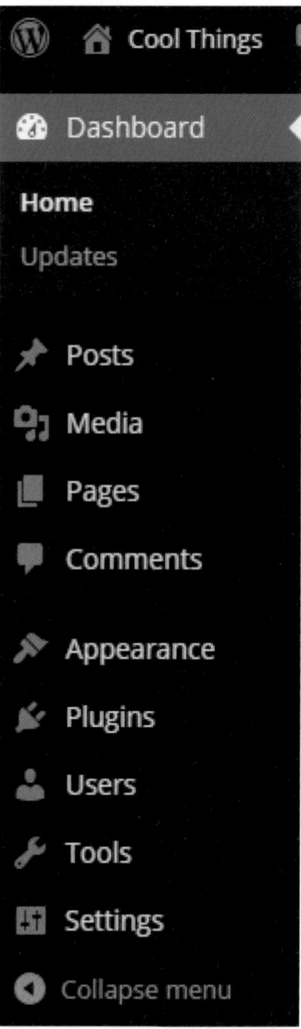

Dashboard

If you hover your mouse on the dashboard menu items, a dropdown list will appear which contains two options: Home and Updates. Clicking on **Home** will take you back to the main dashboard, while clicking on the **Updates** link will take you to a new page where all the pending updates will be displayed.

Posts

The Posts section in WordPress allows you to add, edit, delete and publish posts on your website. You can also put these into categories. The process of creating and publishing posts is explained in Chapter 4.

Media

This item is used to add any media file such as an image, an audio file or a video file to your website media library. You can also view your current Library here. If you hover your mouse over this item, you will see two options appear: Library and Add New.

Pages

This option is used to add new pages to your WordPress site or to edit or update existing pages. Hovering your mouse over this option displays a new menu with two options: All Pages and Add New.

Comments

This section allows you to moderate comments posted on your website. If a user decides to post a comment on any of your posts or pages, then it will appear in this section. You can choose to approve, unapprove, mark as spam or move the comment to the bin.

Appearance

This is the section of WordPress where you can set out the look and feel of your website. Here you can add new themes, customize your current theme, create menus and deal with widgets. This section is explained in more detail in Chapter 3.

Plugins

This menu item can be used to edit installed plugins, remove plugins, activate and deactivate them and also add new plugins. If you hover your mouse over the **Plugins** menu item, you will see a new menu appear with three options: **Installed Plugins**, **Add New** and **Editor**. Plugins are covered in Chapter 5.

When adding new plugins to WordPress, you might discover new links being added to your Dashboard.

Users

This is the option that you can use to add, edit and update roles of the registered and authorized users of your website. You can update things like passwords, and role types for each user. You can even make amendments to your own profile.

Tools

This option is basically used to import and export available tools that can be integrated to your website and enhance its functionality. Tools available here vary according to your host and domain provider.

Settings

The Settings panel is located at the bottom of the menu. It contains all the settings related to content writing, reading, commenting on the posts, links and media settings and most importantly the general settings of your website.

Collapse Menu

This will collapse the dashboard menu options, so you can work without distractions.

Introducing Users

The Users section is where you can add and delete users, as well as edit their user privileges. This is extremely helpful if you have other users working on your website, whether it be writing content for you or developing the site further. To access the User area, click **Users** from the menu on the left hand side.

Before you start creating users, let's have a look at the various roles that you are able to assign to users of your website.

- **Administrator**
  Administrators have complete control over the WordPress site. They can perform all tasks in the WordPress Dashboard, they have complete control over content, and they can do things like change themes, add plugins etc.

- **Editor**
  The role of the Editor is very much the same as it would be with a magazine. They can control all content and moderate comments. However, they can't change the appearance, add any plugins etc.

- **Author**
  The Author can publish, edit or delete their own posts and upload their own media. However, they cannot access material created by other users. They are also unable to create or delete pages.

- **Contributor**
  Contributors can write and edit their own posts. However, the posts will need to be approved by an Administrator or Editor before being published.

- **Subscriber**
  This is the default role for all new user signups. Subscribers can read content and post comments but have no other privileges.

Adding Users

1. To add a new user, start by clicking **Users** > **Add New**

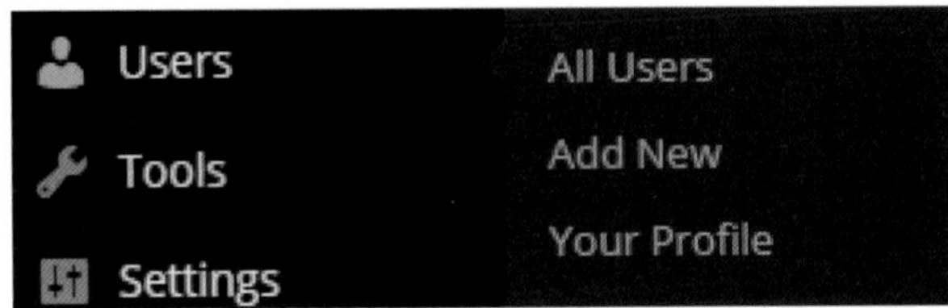

2. You will be presented with a form to fill out for the user. Create a username for the new user, which they will log in with, also add in their Email Address, First Name, Last Name, Website, and a Password. You can choose to send the login details to the user by ticking the box

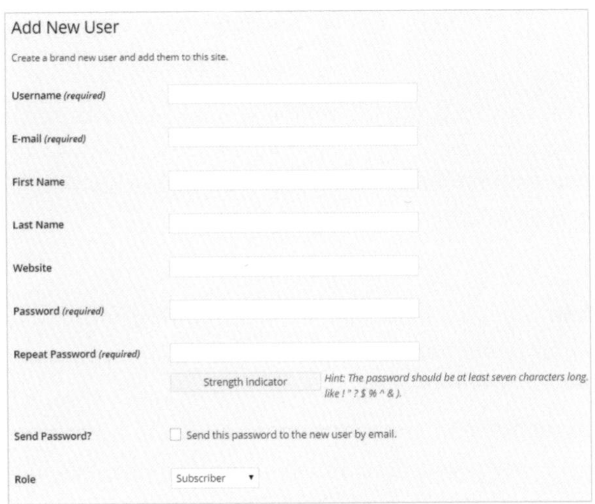

3. Make sure you select the Role from the dropdown box

4. Finally, click **Add New User**. The user can now log in to WordPress using the same login address (**www.yourdomain.com/wp-admin/**)

Add New User

Only give Administrator privileges to people who need it and also make sure you trust them.

Changing User Roles

There may come a time where you want to give another user extra or restricted privileges. To change this go to the **Users** page.

1. Start by clicking **Users > All Users**

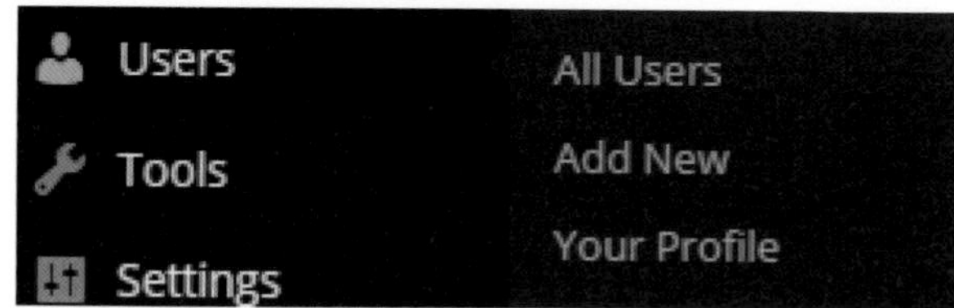

2. Click **"Edit"** underneath the name of the user you want to edit

Edit Link

3. Scroll down until you find the dropdown labeled **Role** and select the new role for the user

4. Remember to click **Update User** at the bottom of the page when you have finished making changes

Color Schemes

There are a number of other things you can change in this section for other users or even yourself. You can change the color scheme for the Dashboard.

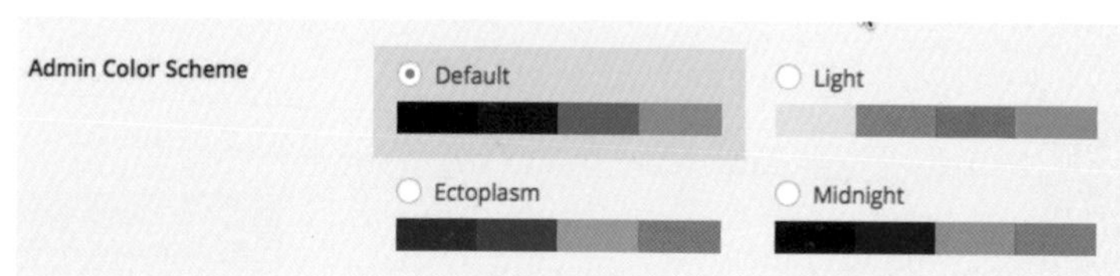

3 Appearance & Themes

This chapter introduces you to Themes, and how you can install, upload and customize them. Themes are an important part of how your website looks.

Introduction to Themes

Web Development: From technicalities to user friendliness

In the early days of the Internet, designing and developing websites was considered a complicated task. There was a common perception that only technical professionals and people with extraordinary IQs could dig into the world of website development. This perception was true to some extent since at that time web development required writing down code and implementing algorithms in editors as simple as a word-processor. However, it is said that change is the only constant. This rule applies to the web development industry as well.

Keeping in view huge advantages associated with marketing and advertising through websites, web developers started developing platforms which can help people develop a website without much programming expertise. Content management systems (CMSs) laid the foundation for such user-friendly web development platforms and WordPress is one of those CMSs.

Where do Themes fit in?

WordPress allows the layman user to develop sophisticated and professional-looking websites without any prior knowledge of programming, via Themes.

Simply put, a WordPress Theme is basically a pre-built, database-driven web template which can be tweaked and modified to fit the needs of a desired website. There are thousands of WordPress Themes out there, some of which are free, but you can also pay extra for premium offerings. Experienced developers will create their own themes from scratch. This is something we will cover on pages 166-174.

A Theme is composed of several components, some of which are common while others are intrinsic to themes. Common components of a Theme include Menus, Widgets and Headers. You can change your Theme at any time during the development of your website without having to worry about any content changing. Once a theme is activated, the look of your website will automatically change.

Adding Themes

To add a theme to a WordPress site:

1. Log in to the dashboard of your WordPress website or blog

2. In the Dashboard, find Appearance and click Themes

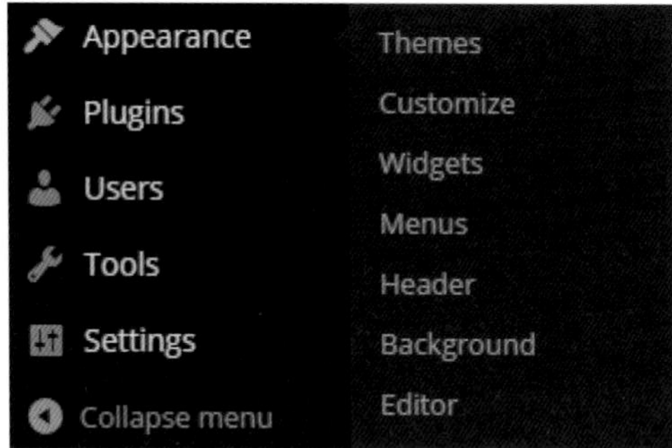

You should then be presented with a screen (similar to the one below), which shows Themes already installed. At the top of the page there is a search box where you can search already-added Themes in your blog, as well as an **Add New** button where you can add new Themes to WordPress.

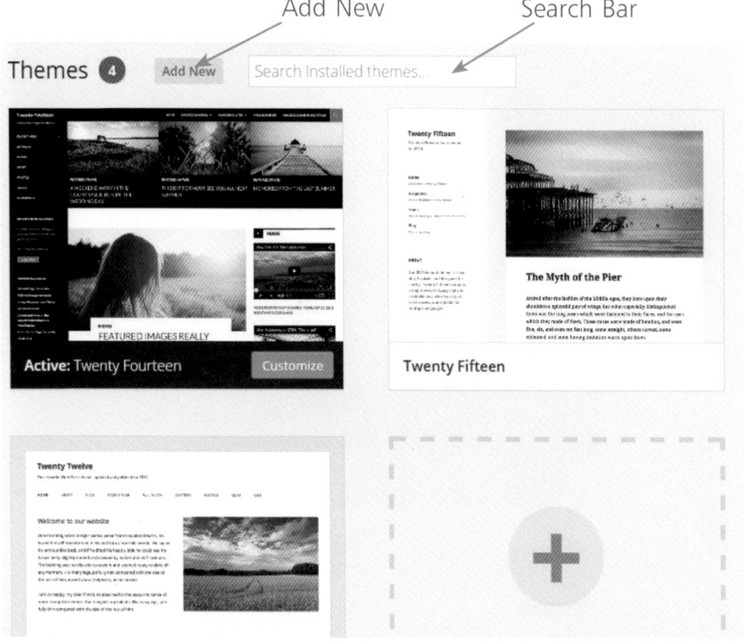

...cont'd

3. To begin adding a new Theme, click **Add New**

You will then be presented with a screen, where you can browse through a number of new Themes. These include **Featured**, **Popular** and **Latest**. There is also a section called **Feature Filter** where you can browse for Themes based on your Feature requirements. There is also a search bar where you can enter the name of a Theme.

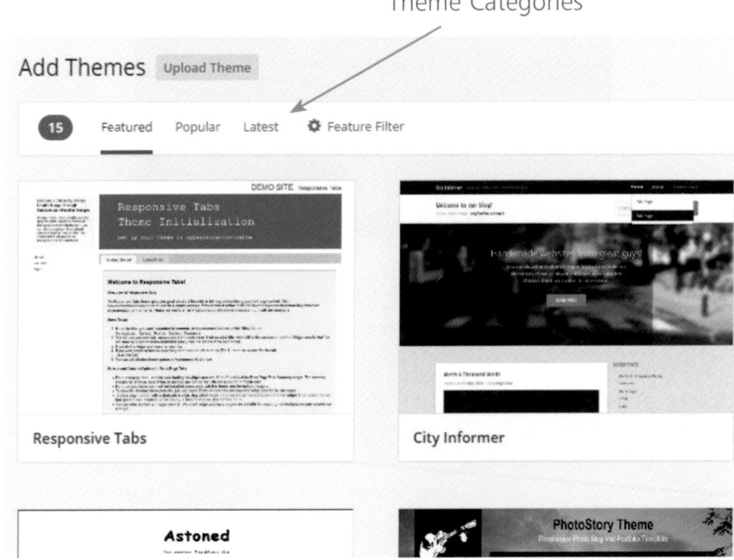

If you hover your mouse on one of the Themes, you can choose to preview the Theme without installing, or you can install the Theme by clicking the **Install** button.

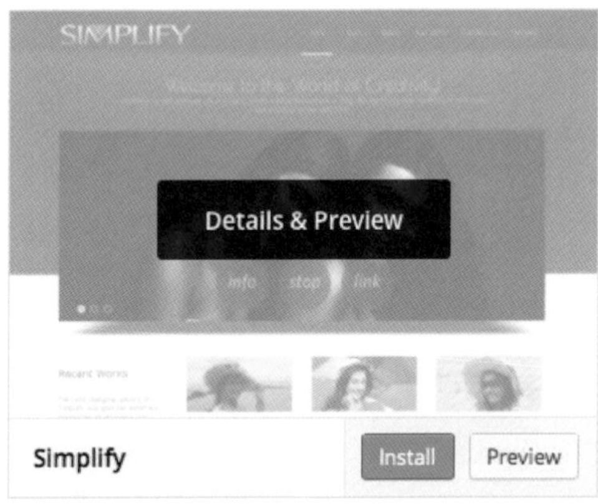

Once you click the **Install** button, the Theme you selected will be installed and you will be redirected to a new page

Installing Theme: City Informer

Downloading install package from https://wordpress.

Unpacking the package...

Installing the theme...

Successfully installed the theme **City Informer 1.3.**

Live Preview | Activate | Return to Theme Installer

Live Preview, Activate and Return to Theme Installer

You can have more than one Theme installed. However, only one can be activated at a time.

Once installation has completed, you have three options at the bottom. These options are **Live Preview**, **Activate** and **Return to Theme Installer**.

Clicking **Live Preview** will show you a live preview of your website with the theme you selected, but it will not activate the Theme, so it gives you a chance to decide whether or not you like the look of your Theme with your current content. Clicking the **Activate** link will activate the Theme. Now, if you visit your website, you will see the new theme applied to your site. If you decide to click **Return to Theme Installer,** it will take you back to the page where you can re-select from a number of Themes.

Deleting a Theme

Deleting a Theme is an extremely simple process. Go back to **Appearance** > **Themes** and click on the Theme you wish to delete. A new page appears displaying Theme details. In the bottom right corner, there is a link to delete the Theme.

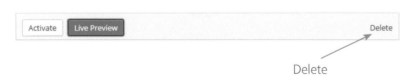

Delete

Activating Themes can change the layout of your content so make sure you are happy with the design before you decide to activate.

When you click **Delete**, you will be asked to confirm that you wish to delete the Theme.

Uploading a Theme

Apart from installing built-in Themes from WordPress.org, you can also buy Themes from other vendors. WordPress has a huge developer community and there are thousands of developers developing extremely cool and fascinating Themes. Besides, you can also develop your own WordPress themes if you have sufficient programming skills in PHP and client-side web development languages.

When you buy or develop a Theme, what you get is a simple zip file that contains all the necessary files that make up a Theme. This zip file is then uploaded to your WordPress blog or site. To upload a new Theme to WordPress:

1. Log in to the Dashboard of your WordPress blog or website
2. From the menu in the Dashboard, click **Appearance > Themes**

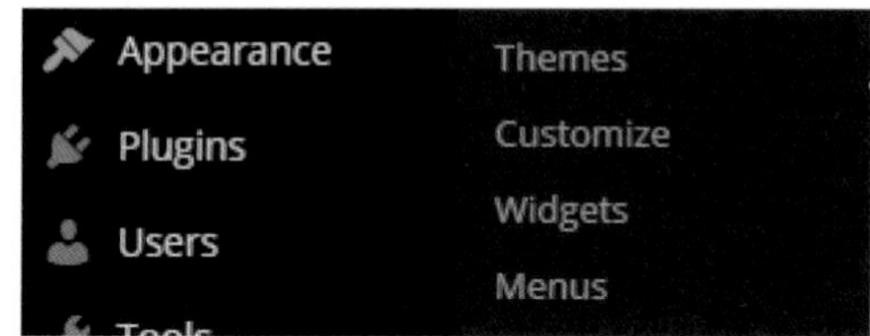

3. Click **Add New**
4. Click **Upload Theme** instead of selecting from any of the WordPress.org Themes

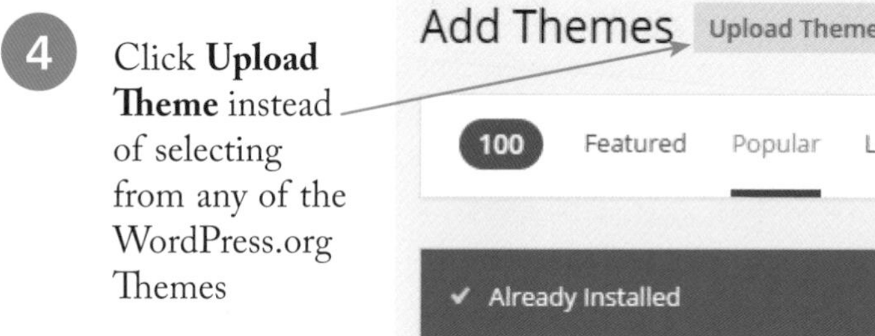

5. Click on the **Choose File** button. A new file dialogue will open for you to locate the zip file that includes your Theme. Once you have located the file, click the **Choose** button from the file dialogue

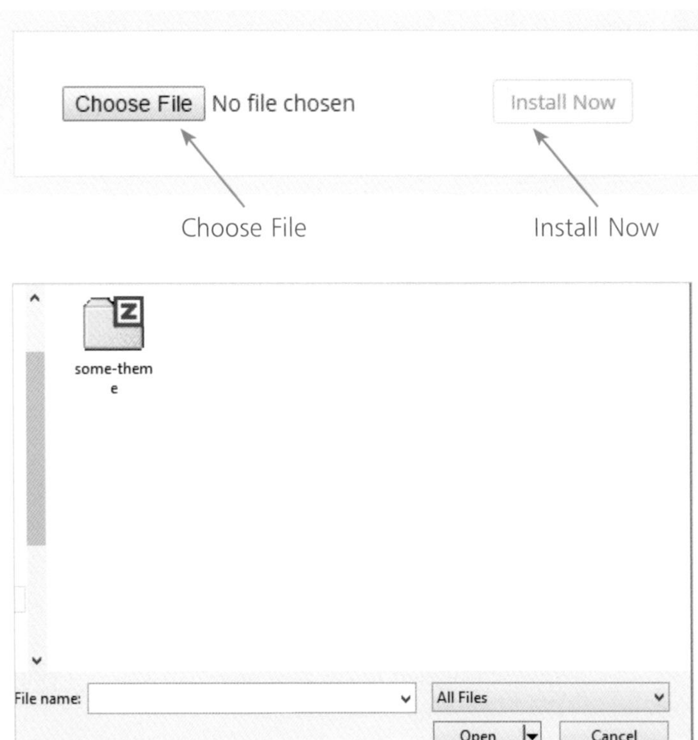

6. Once you click the **Install Now** button, a new screen will be displayed showing the installation process. This is very similar to the one shown when adding a Theme from the WordPress.org library (see page 33)

The activation process is also similar. Once again, you will get the three options of **Live Preview**, **Activate** and **Return to Theme Installer.** You simply have to click the **Activate** link at the end of the installation information and the process is complete.

Customize Your Theme

WordPress Themes come with several default options such as tagline, header image, background color etc. However, the default Theme options can be customized via the WordPress admin dashboard. To customize WordPress Theme options:

1. Log in to the Dashboard of your WordPress blog or website

2. From the menu in the Dashboard, click **Appearance > Customize**

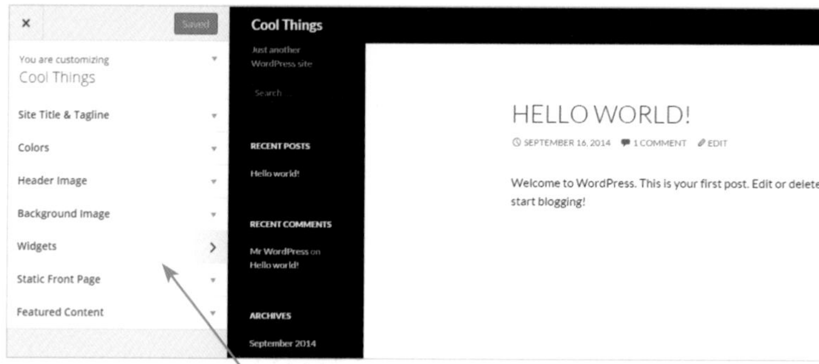

Customizable Options

You will notice a number of customizable options down the left-hand side along with a web preview down on the right-hand side. This will update everytime you make a change. The options you get will depend on the Theme you have selected.

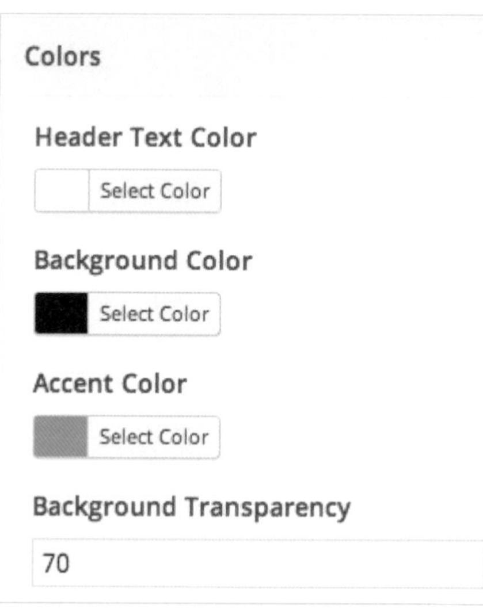

For example, here you can customize the header text color, background color, accent color etc.

You can select the color scheme for those particular elements. There are other elements you can customize too.

Once you have finished click **Save & Publish** to update the live website.

Customizing Menus

Menus are usually located at the top of your page or side bar, depending upon the Theme you chose. They usually display a number of links allowing the user to easily navigate through each page of your website. Always remember that your website can have multiple menus.

1. From the Dashboard, click **Appearance** > **Menus**

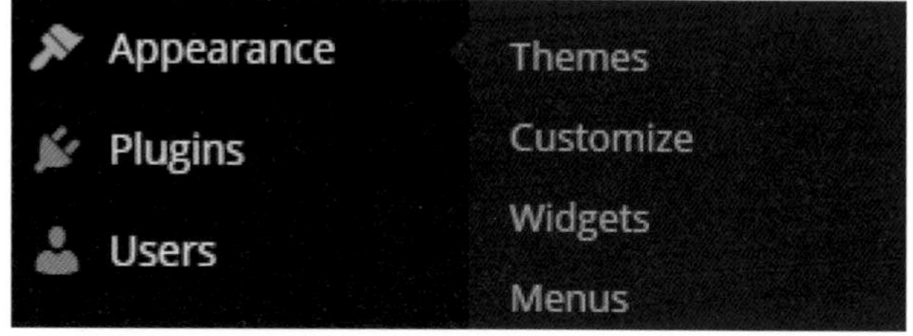

Under the Menu Structure, the default Menu is displayed that shows already added menu items along with their types. Your already-added pages might be different to the one shown in the above screenshot, depending upon the Theme you chose. However, the process of adding new menu items and creating items is similar.

2. On the left-hand side will be a list of pages that you have already created. To select one or more of those, check the tick boxes next to them

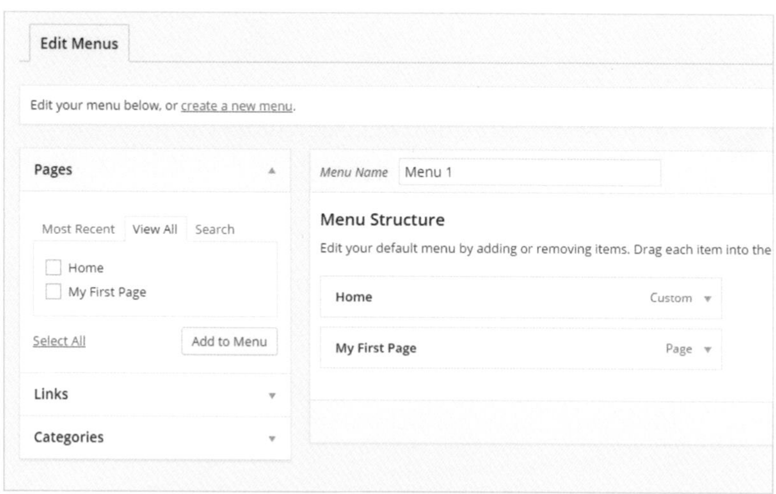

...cont'd

Hot tip

You can have more than one menu on your website. You are not just restricted to one. Some Themes will already have a second one built in.

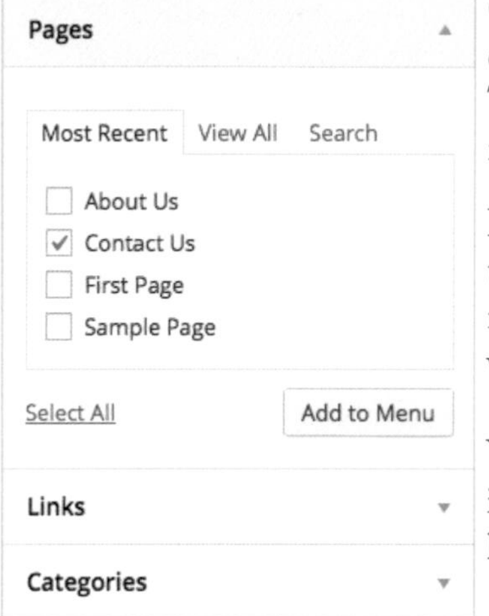

Once you have selected the pages, click the **Add to Menu** button. This will add the pages to the menu structure.

In this example, I have selected the **Contact Us** page, which means this would be the item that will be added to the menu.

You may have a different list of items, depending on what pages have been created.

3. Now, if you go to your blog or website's main page, you will see that your newly-added item has been added to your menu

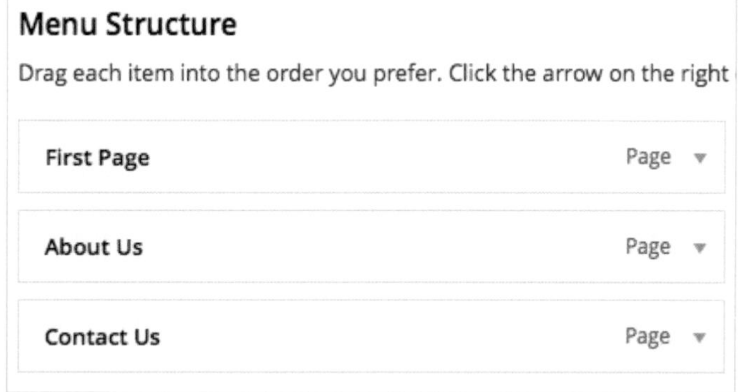

4. In the Menu Structure, you can reorder the pages by selecting an item and dragging it above or below another menu item

5. You can also add external links to your menu. All you need to do is select the Links section on the left hand side

   Link URL: The URL of the page you want to link to
   Link Text: This is how you want the link name to appear

Adding Widgets

Widgets are small applications that enhance user experience and responsiveness, and provide additional functionalities other than built-in Theme features. A really cool demonstration of a Widget is a Facebook Like Box which is often displayed on the homepage of a website. A Facebook Like Box displays the number of people who have liked the page, and the user can also like the page directly from the Like Box instead of finding the page on Facebook and then liking that.

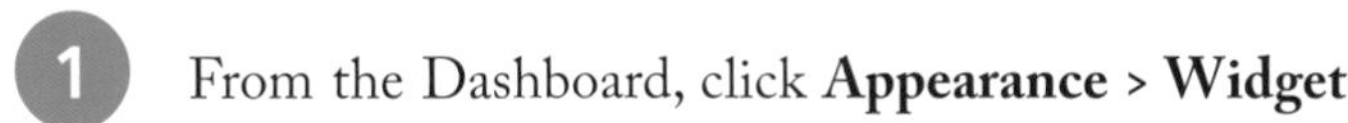

1 From the Dashboard, click **Appearance** > **Widgets**

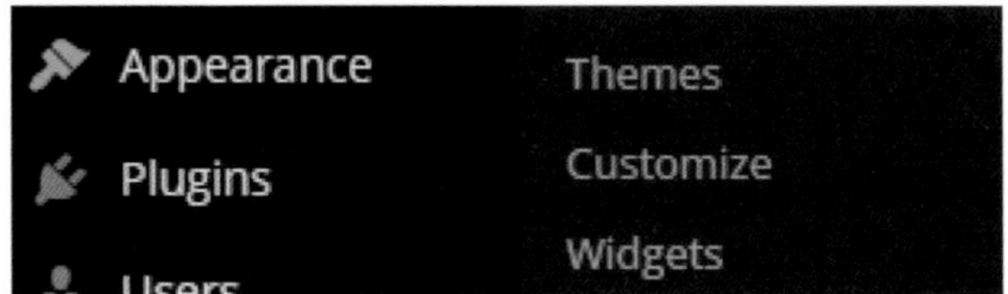

Something very similar to the screenshot below will appear. This again will vary by Theme. You may find you have more widget areas to choose from. **Available Widgets** will appear on the left, and the **Widget Areas** will appear on the right.

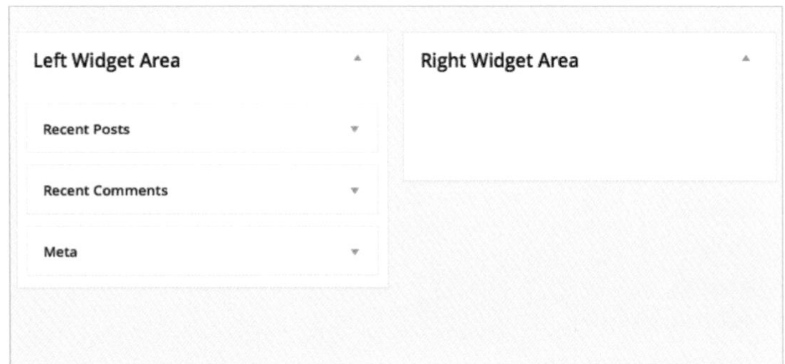

The Left Widget Area is already filled with three widgets **Recent Posts**, **Recent Comments** and **Meta**.

2 Drag the **Recent Comments** Widget from the Available Widgets area and put it in the **Right Widget Area**

When adding new plugins (see Chapter Five), you will sometimes have new Widgets appear relevant to that plugin. For example – if you add a Twitter plugin, then you may see a Twitter widget appear allowing you to display Tweets.

...cont'd

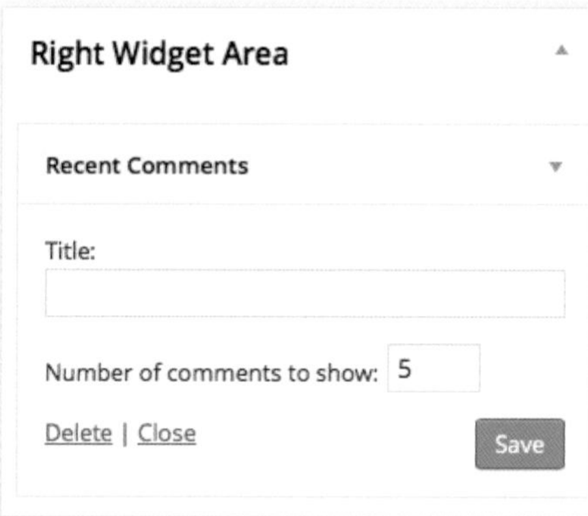

3. You are now faced with some options for that Widget. In this example, add a title and enter the number of comments you want to show. Let's say 1 and click **Save**

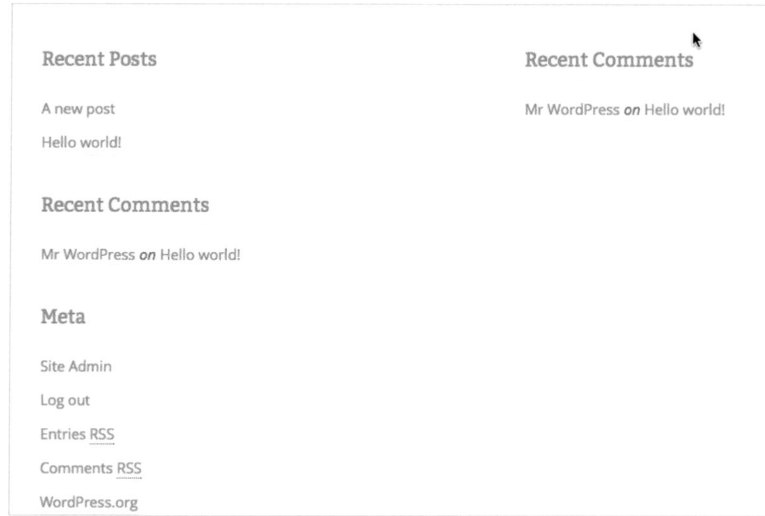

You will now notice on the live site that Recent Comments has appeared on the right-hand side. This is a very basic example – you can get some very good widgets, either through plugins (see Chapter Five), or by using external sites that provide code to paste inside the Text widget.

To add a Facebook Like Box Widget:

You can go back to Facebook to edit your Like Box at any time. There are various Facebook plugins on offer too.

1. Visit **https://developers.facebook.com/docs/plugins/like-box-for-pages**

2. You can customize the height, color scheme and URL of the Facebook page. It will give you an instant preview of how your box will look

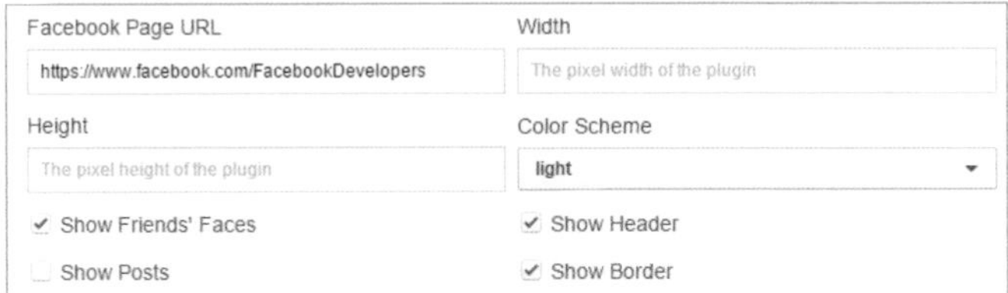

3. Once you are finished, click **Get Code** right at the bottom of the page

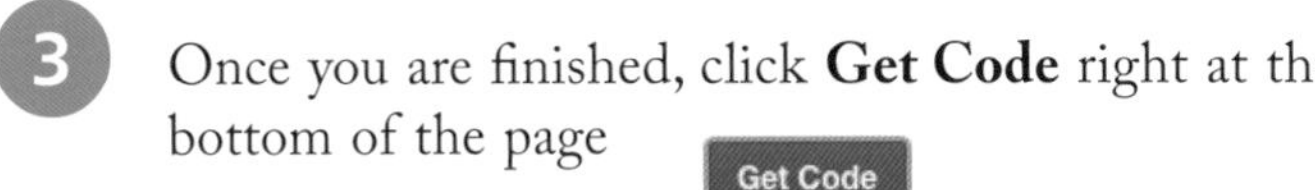

4. Copy the plugin code that you are given

5. Now, go back to the Widgets page, and drag a "Text" widget over from Available Widgets across to the Right Widget Area

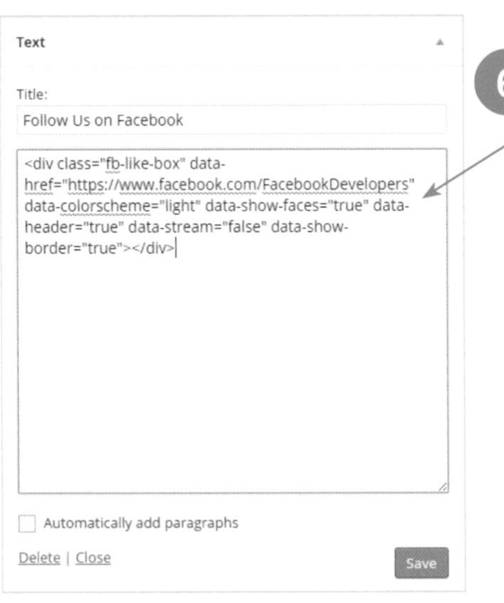

6. Paste your code into this box. This will then set up your Facebook Widget on the right-hand side. Don't forget to click **Save**!

Your page should now display the Facebook Widget.

The Editor

With sufficient programming knowledge of CSS3, HTML, JavaScript and PHP, you can easily edit already-developed CSS Themes. WordPress provides built-in functionality for editing Themes via Editor. To edit WordPress Themes:

Beware

Be careful when altering PHP files, as you could end up causing damage to your website. Proceed with caution!

From the menus in the Dashboard, click **Appearance > Editor**

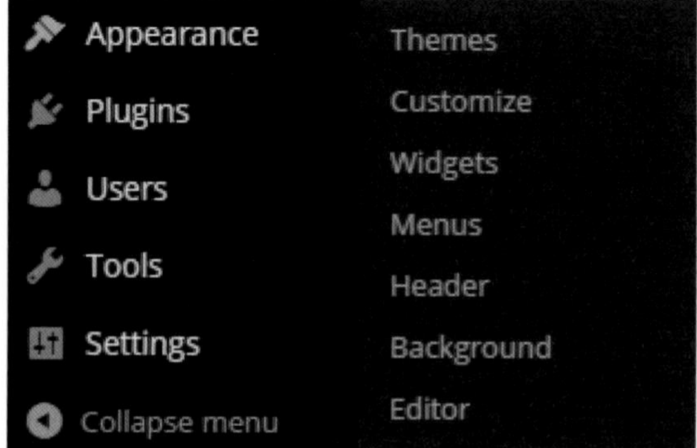

The page that appears contains all the pages, styles, functionalities and virtually every component of the Theme.

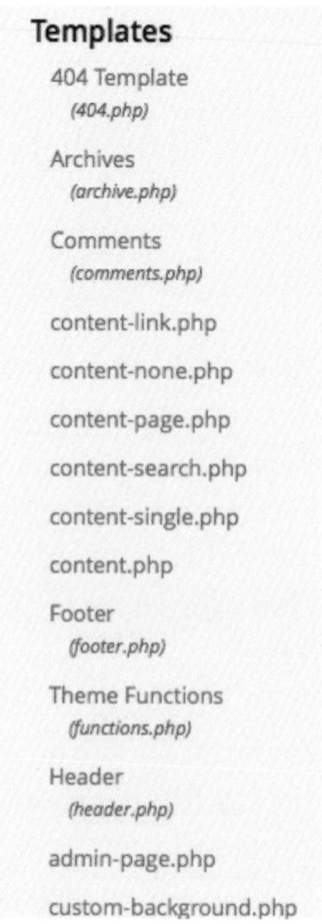

The pages, style sheets and script appear on the right sidebar. You can choose any page to edit from the right side bar. Once you click any page, the content of the page will appear in the center window where you can make changes in the code.

2. Once you have made your changes, click the **Update File** button at the bottom of the document and your file will be updated. This area is more for experienced developers – if you consider editing any templates, then it is best to have an FTP account set up so you can constantly make backup and changes very easily

Any Theme can be edited from this area, this adds flexibility, giving experienced developers the opportunity to extend their website even further.

4 Creating Content

This chapter introduces you to Pages and Posts. It will also walk you through adding content, such as text, images, videos and audio.

Pages & Posts Differences

What is the difference between a WordPress page and a post? This is one of the most common questions asked by entry level WordPress developers, but it's not hard to understand. Once you log in to your WordPress blog or website, you will see two separate options on your dashboard for Posts and Pages.

The screenshot below highlights both Pages and Posts and their location in the Dashboard.

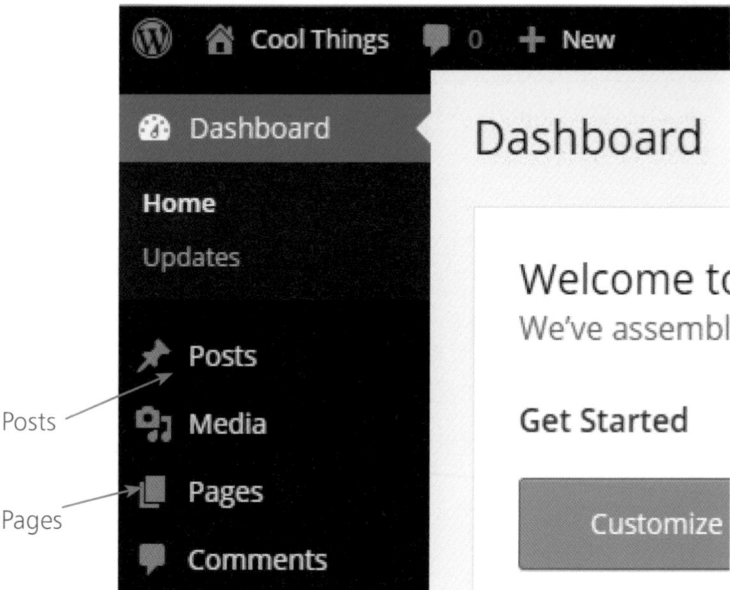

Let us have a look at the major differences between a WordPress page and a post.

What is a Page?

Whenever you visit the homepage of a website, you see multiple options on the menu-bar which is mostly located at the top of the homepage. The menu-bar contains options such as Home, About Us, Services, Contact us etc.

When you click any of these options, you are taken to another page which contains details of the option you selected.

For instance, if you select the Services option from the menu bar, you will be taken to the page that contains details of the services offered by the company. The same holds true for Contact Us and other options. Basically, these options represent an individual, dedicated page.

Usually a page contains static content which is not likely to change for long periods of time. The content of the page is usually not required to be updated too often.

For instance, your About Us page is unlikely to change frequently. In simple words, it can be said of pages that they are timeless entities. Though the backend database stores the date of publication of the page, you will not usually see the publication date of a page's content.

A page usually doesn't contain social media buttons. For instance, you might prefer that your privacy policy is not shared on Facebook or Twitter etc. Also, comments are disabled on pages.

What is a Post?

Posts are entries on your website that are listed in reverse order of time of publication. Latest posts appear at the top of the page and older posts appear down the page. Posts are bound with time. Therefore, posts can be retrieved based on year and month. Since posts are time-bound entities, they can be delivered via RSS feeds to the subscribers.

Another important consideration regarding posts is that comments are allowed under the posts. Posts are meant to foster healthy discussions. Therefore, social media icons are also enabled alongside posts so that readers can directly share the content of the post on their social media profiles. When viewing a post you will see the following information:

- Post Title
- Category
- Author
- Date Posted

RSS stands for Really Simple Syndication. It's a way for you to easily distribute a list of headlines, update notices and sometimes content to a wide number of people.

Creating a Page

Creating a page in WordPress is a simple process. Following are the steps that need to be performed in order to create a page in WordPress:

1. Log in into your WordPress blog/website with admin credentials

2. On the dashboard, hover your mouse over the Pages option. A new menu appears containing two options: All Pages and Add New. Click on the **Add New** option

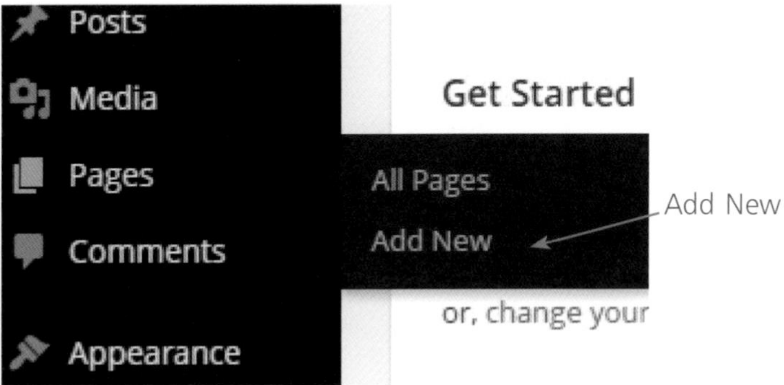

3. After you click the Add New option, a new window appears where the title of the new page and the content can be entered. In the screenshot below, **My First Page** is the title of the page, followed by the text of the page in the Editor

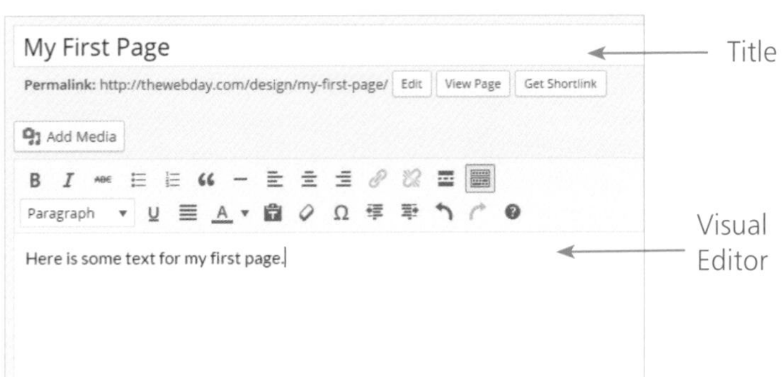

4. Click on the **Publish** button on the right hand side of the page to publish the page. Clicking publish will make your newly created page go live. You can also choose to save a draft of your work by clicking **Save Draft.** If you wish to preview your current page at this time, click on the **Preview** button

You can save a draft of your page instead of publishing instantly, so you can finish the page at a later date.

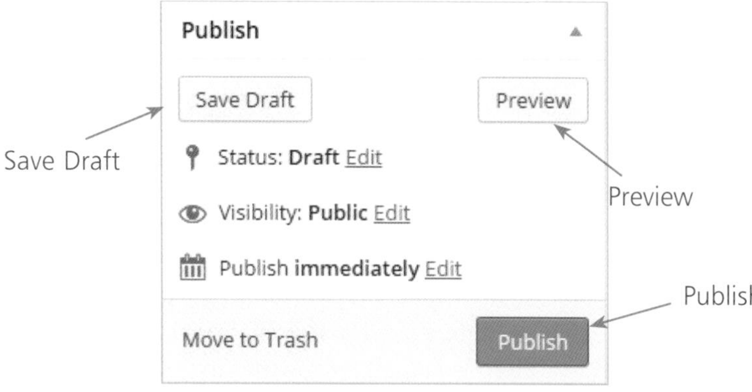

5. Now, if you go to **Pages > All Pages**, you will find that your newly created page has been added to the list of pages contained by your website/blog as shown in the screenshot below

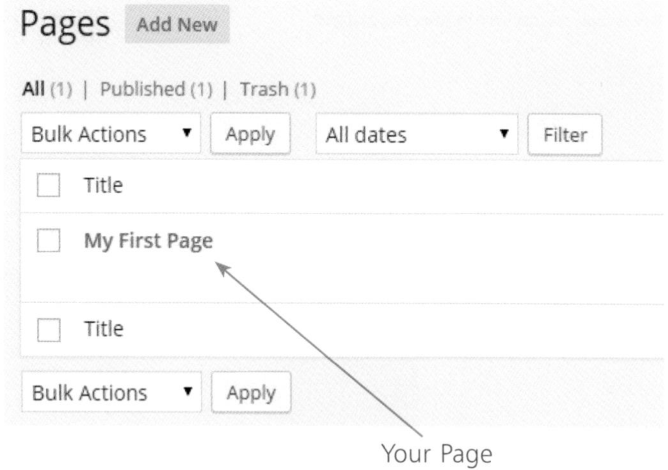

Creating a Post

Creating a post is very similar to creating a page. Follow the steps below to create a post in WordPress:

1. Log in to the Dashboard of your blog and hover your mouse over **Posts**. It will expand a menu towards right. Click on **Add New** from the expanded menu

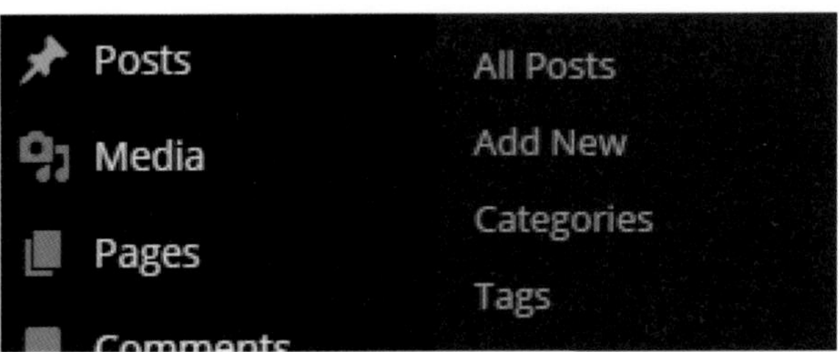

2. In the window that appears, enter the title of the post, and in the Visual Editor enter the content of the post. In this example, "My First Post" is the title of the post, followed by "Here is some text for my first post. Happy days!" in the Visual Editor

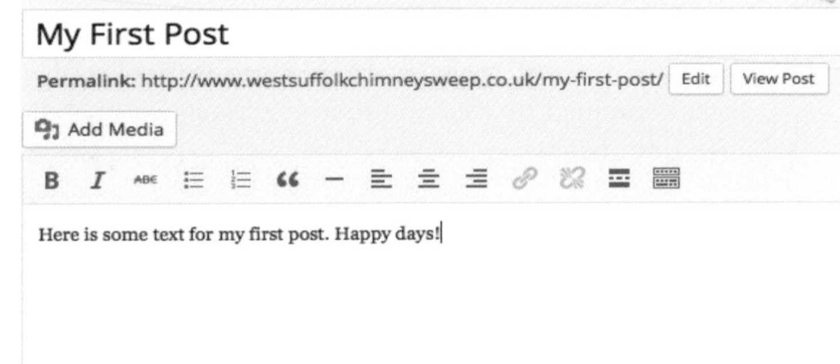

3. In order to publish the post, you simply have to click the **Publish** button located to the right, the same as publishing a page. You can also **Save Draft** or **Preview** from here

Try to keep backups of your pages and posts on your local machine in a Word document or text document.

Adding Text

Adding text to a post/page is very simple. Now that you have learned how to create pages and posts, you are ready to start adding content.

1. Let's start by loading up the post we just created. Click **Posts** and then click **My First Post**

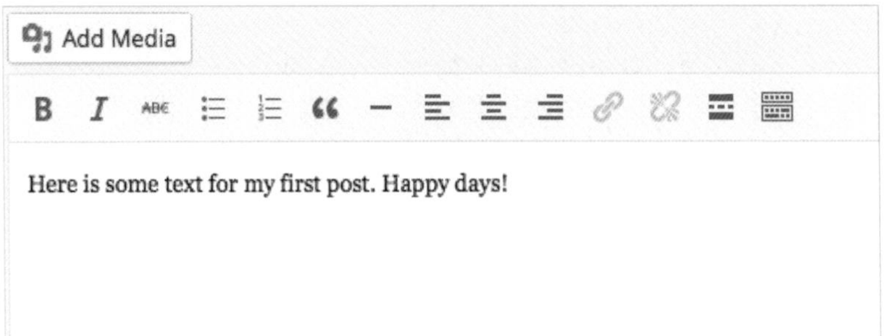

Let's have a look at the editor once again. You will notice in the screenshot above, there is a large space for visual editor. In here you can add your content whether it be text or images. We will move onto images shortly, but first let's focus on text. You can insert text into here like you can with any good word processor. You will notice there are two tabs on the right hand side of the visual editor (Visual and Text) as shown in the screenshot below.

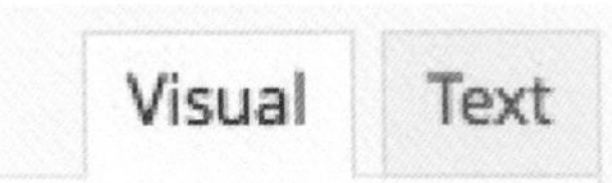

2. Make sure that the Visual Tab is selected as this is where you will type in your content. You would really only use the Text Tab if you were going to enter custom HTML code (explained on page 42)

3. Add your own text in the box

...cont'd

Just above the visual editor you will notice a toolbar as shown below. This allows you to customize your text. For example, Bold, Underline, Create a Link etc.

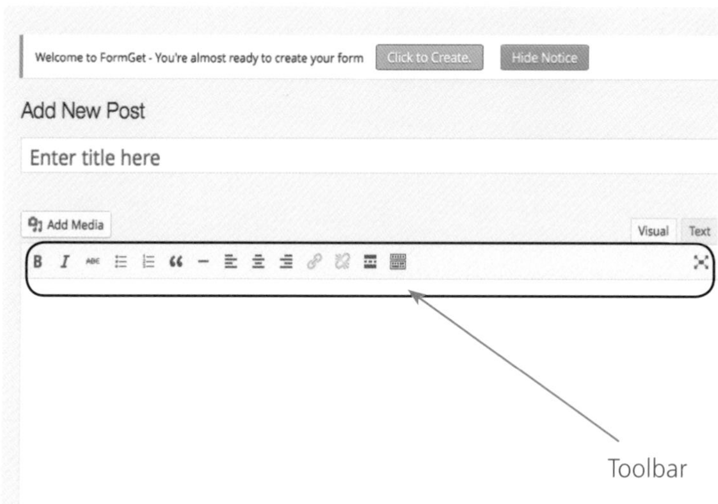

Using the text toolbar is a great way of formatting your text in WordPress.

Here is an explanation of each of the elements:

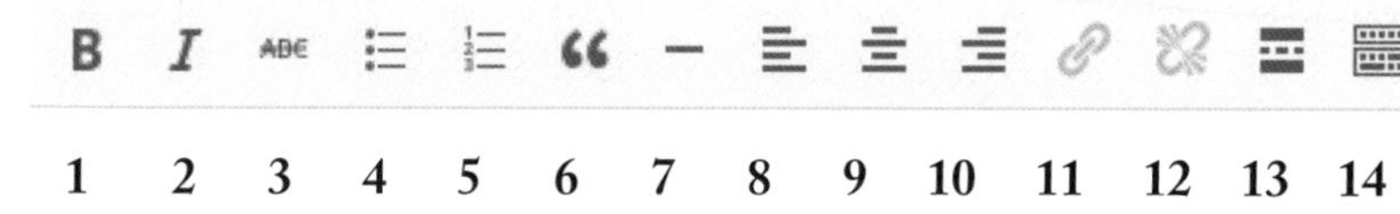

1 2 3 4 5 6 7 8 9 10 11 12 13 14

1. Bold
2. Italic
3. Strikethrough
4. Bullet Point List
5. Numbered List
6. Block Quote: Each theme will display this differently
7. Horizontal Line
8. Align Text Left
9. Center Text
10. Align Text Right
11. Insert Link
12. Unlink
13. Insert More Tag
14. Enables Second Row of Toolbar

You will see this option right on the end of the toolbar. It allows distraction-free writing by entering the full screen mode.

If you click number 14 (on the previous page), this will bring up a second row of tools (shown below) that you can also use to format your text:

1 2 3 4 5 6 7 8 9 10 11 12

Sometimes the full set of both toolbars will automatically appear. This varies on installation.

Here are what the second set of elements do:

1. This dropdown box gives you a set of text styles
2. Underlines text
3. Justifies text
4. Changes text colour
5. Pastes text
6. Clear formatting for that set of text
7. Allows you to add a special character
8. Decreases Indent
9. Increases Indent
10. Undo your last action
11. Redo your last action
12. Brings up the keyboard shortcuts

After doing some alterations to your text using the visual editor, you may want to check out the code behind it. Click **Text**. It will show you the HTML code for what you have written and formatted.

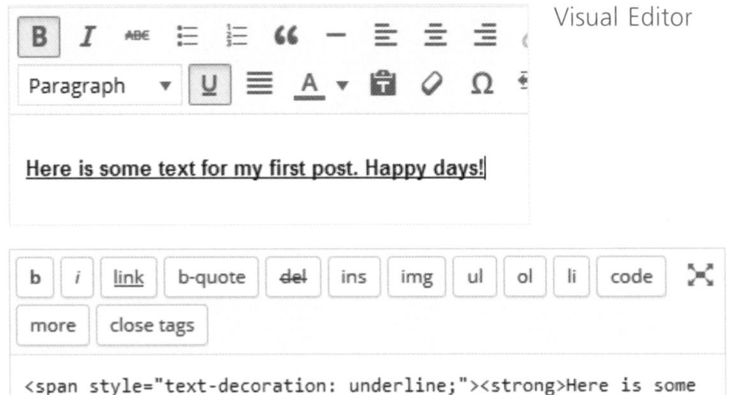

Visual Editor

Text Editor

Do not add HTML code unless you are familar with the language.

Adding Images

We all want our websites to look great, and what better way to tell a story than adding media to your pages. Adding images to a page is extremely straightforward.

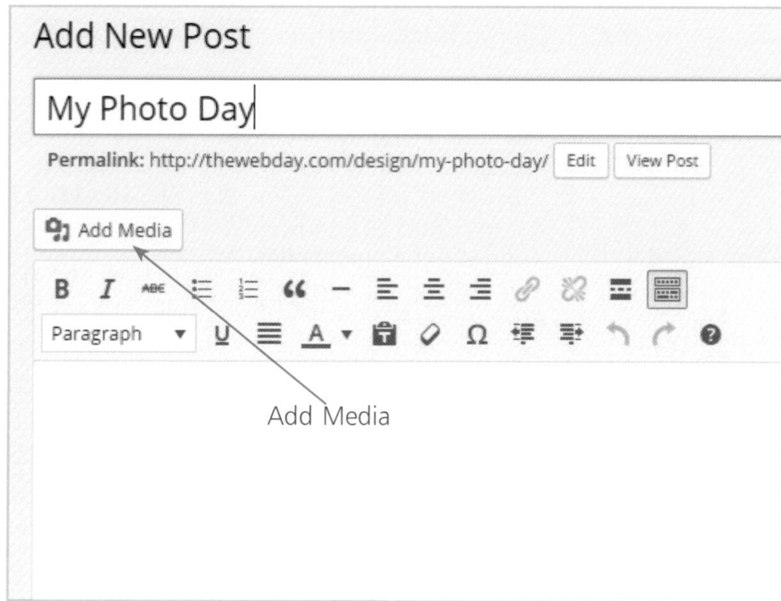

First let's have a look at how to upload your own images to WordPress and insert them into your Page.

1. To get started, place the cursor on your Page at the location where you want to add the media. Click on **Add Media** button. You will have two options:

- **Upload Media:** This allows you to upload media you have saved on your computer
- **Media Library:** This will allow you to select media that you have already uploaded to WordPress

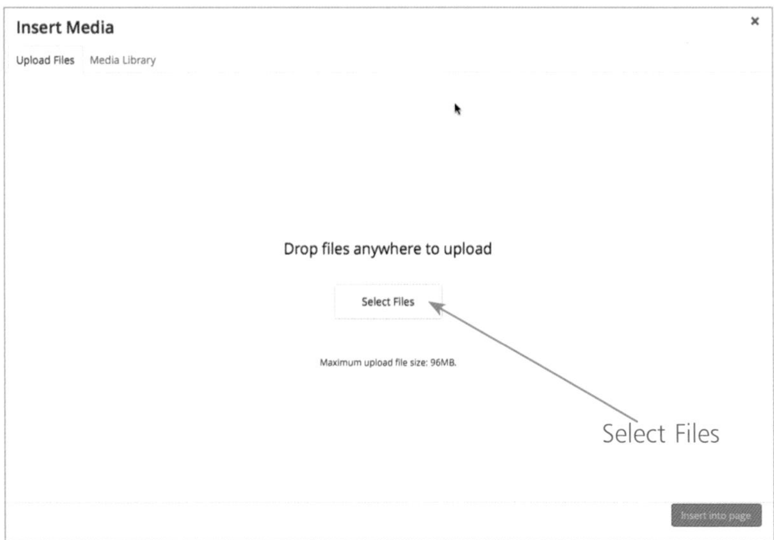

2 Drop your media into this window if you wish, or you can click the **Select Files** button. This will bring up a dialog box which will allow you to select the media files of your choice from your computer

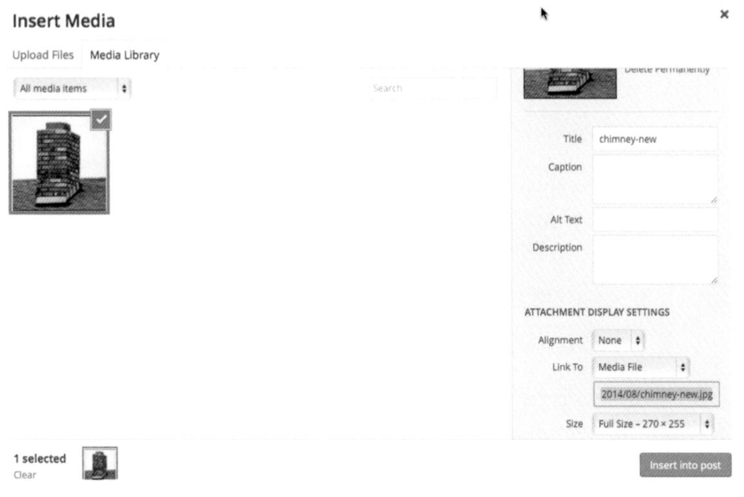

The image that you have uploaded will automatically be added to the Media Library.

...cont'd

3. Now that you have chosen the image from your computer, you will be presented with a few options on the right-hand side

ATTACHMENT DETAILS
chimney-new.jpg
August 13, 2014
270 × 255
Edit Image
Delete Permanently

Title: chimney-new
Caption
Alt Text
Description

ATTACHMENT DISPLAY SETTINGS
Alignment: None
Link To: Media File
http://thewebday.com/wp
Size: Full Size – 270 × 255

Insert into post

Title: Choose a title for the image.
Caption: This caption will appear when you hover over the picture.
Alt Text: If the image does not load on your website, then it will display this text. This is an effective way of telling Google the topic of your page which will boost your search rankings.
Description: A description of the image.
Alignment: How do you want the image to align on your page? Left, Right or Center?
Link To: You can link the image to either the media file itself, a custom URL or an attachment page.
Size: Choose the size of the image. If it's too big you might want to use a smaller size.

4. Click **Insert into post** button when you are ready to add the image to your page or post.

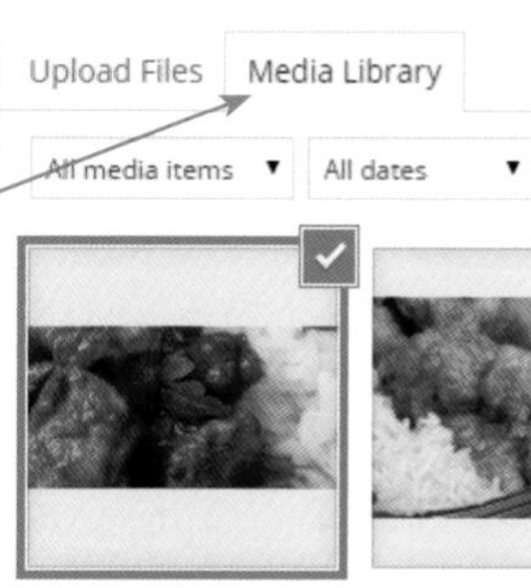

Alternatively, you can select an image from the **Media Library**, which contains all the images you have already uploaded to your website, and media is inserted the same way as above.

Hot tip

Alt Text is also a good way to provide an audio description for those who are visually impaired and use audio describe to hear what is on the screen.

Adding Videos

You will be amazed at just how simple it is to embed YouTube videos on your WordPress website. Videos are becoming much more popular and video blogging is on the rise!

1. Copy the URL of the YouTube video from your browser

https://www.youtube.com/watch?v=nuiHbLxPiHU

2. Create or open up the page or post where you want to add your video

3. Paste the YouTube link in to the Visual Editor, and the video will instantly appear

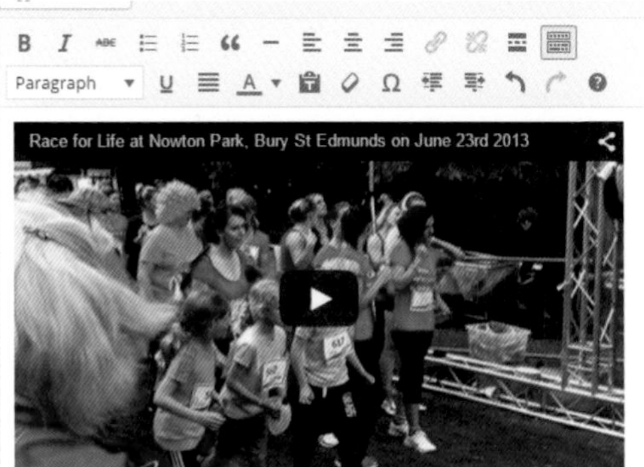

4. Then click **Publish or Update.** You will notice the video is now on your page or post

Adding HTML Code

If you are familiar with HTML code, then you can add code to your pages and posts. HTML is a great way of adding functionality and style to your web pages.

1. Open up a page or post that you have created

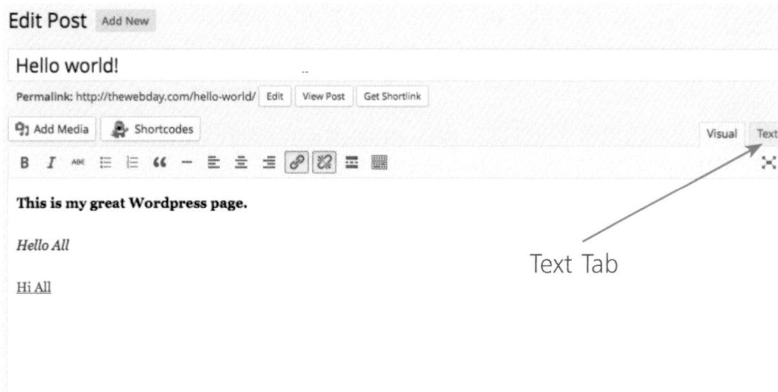

2. Click the **Text** tab as highlighted above

3. You will now be presented with a very similar window to the Visual Editor but this one is used for writing code

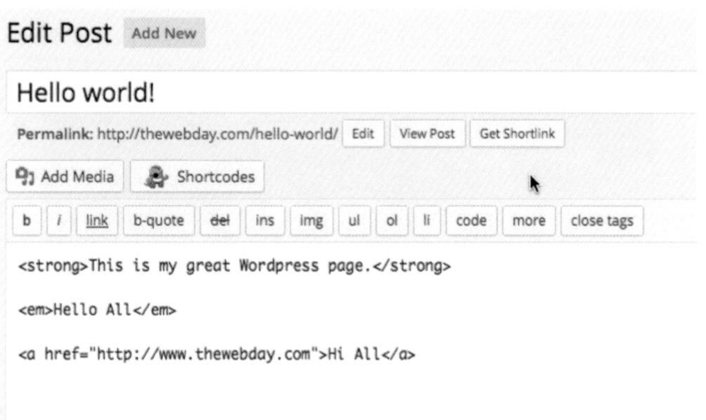

If you have already created content, like adding or formatting text then you should already see some HTML code here. This was automatically created as you added content to the Visual Editor.

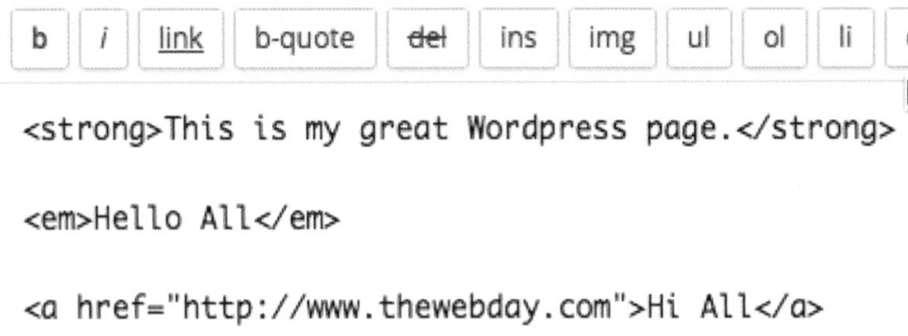

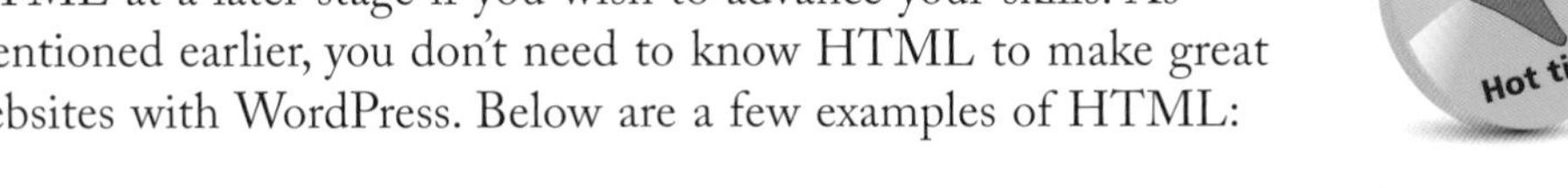

You can add your own code in this window if you wish. Don't worry if you don't understand the code here. You can always learn HTML at a later stage if you wish to advance your skills. As mentioned earlier, you don't need to know HTML to make great websites with WordPress. Below are a few examples of HTML:

Learn more about HTML with HTML5 in easy steps.

Links

<a href ="http://www.thewebday.com">My Link</a>

This will create a hyperlink on the page called "My Link", which will link to the page http://www.thewebday.com.

Text Color

<span style="color: blue;">House</span>

This code will write the word House in the color blue.

Align Text

<p style="text-align: center;">Hello</p>

This code will align the word Hello in the center.

Item List

```
<ul>
        <li>Milk</li>
        <li>Eggs</li>
</ul>
```

This code will create a bullet point list of two items – Milk and Eggs.

Adding Audio

Adding audio to websites has become more popular over the last few years especially with those trying to get their music noticed. Adding audio to your page or post is as simple as adding an image.

1. Load up the page or post where you want to add your audio

2. Click **Add Media** at the top of the page

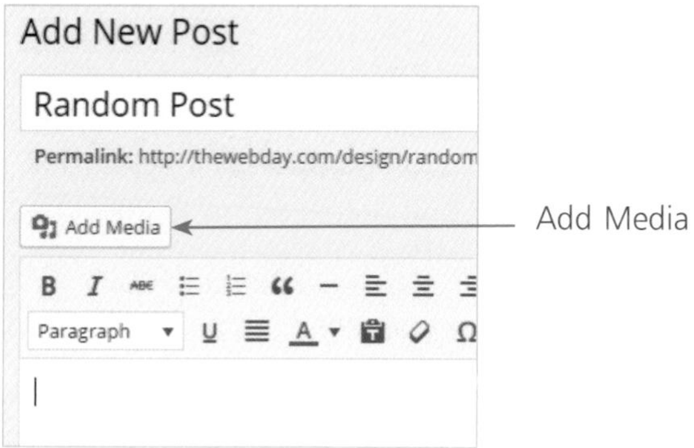

3. Select the music file you want to upload from your PC

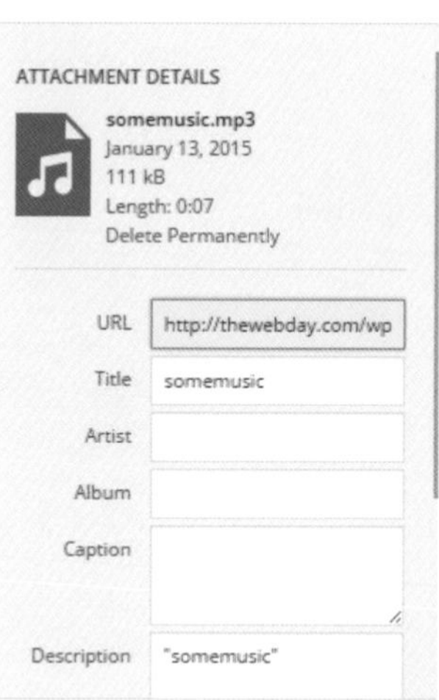

Just like with an image, the attachment details will load.

4. Add the title and description

5. Make sure you select **Embed Media Player** from the dropdown

6. Click **Insert into Post** located at the bottom

The audio file is now embeded into your page or post.

Creating Categories

Posts can be added to categories or sub-categories. Categories are basically a way to group posts. For instance you can create a category named **Web Development** on your blog and add all your web development posts in that category. Usually if you create a post, and don't create a category, then it will go into the Uncategorized category. Creating a category is a simple process.

1. Click **Posts** > **Categories** as shown below

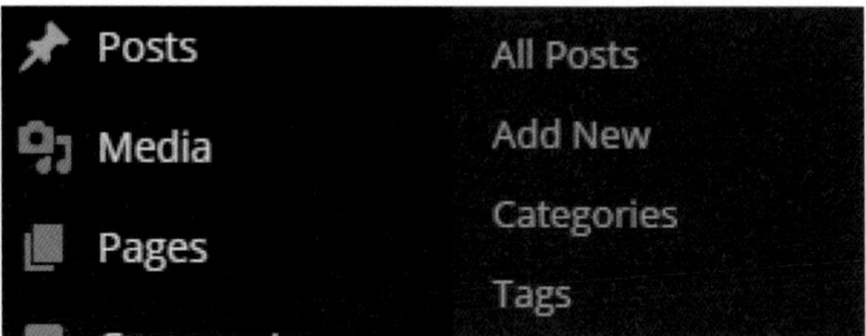

2. A new window appears where you can add the particulars of the new category

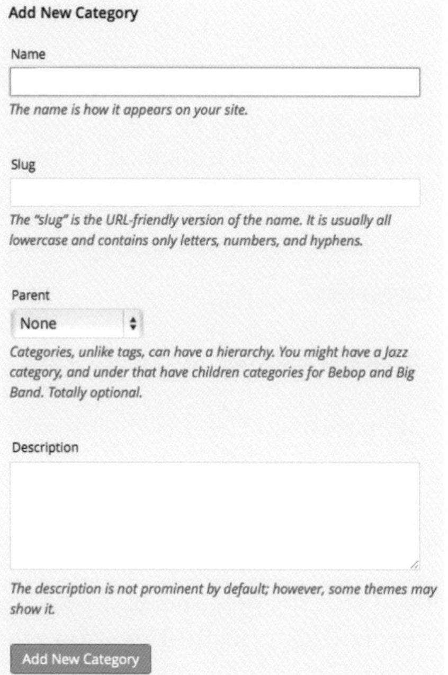

3. In the Name field, enter the name of the new category

...cont'd

4. Enter the Slug value which is the URL-friendly version of the category name – usually lowercase letters, numbers and hyphens. Don't add any spaces

5. From the Parent dropdown list choose **None** as this is your first category. You would only add a parent if you were creating a subcategory. For example, if you had already created a category called Games Consoles and you were creating a new category called Xbox, then you might select Games Consoles as a parent

6. Finally, click **Add New Category** button at the end of the window to create a new Category. The newly added category will show straight away in the list of categories on the right

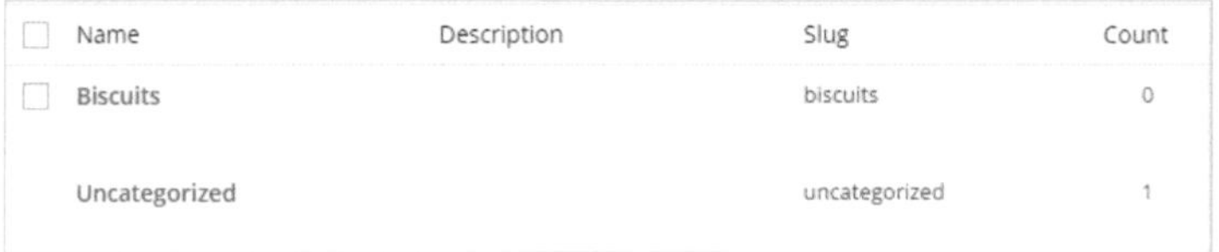

Name	Description	Slug	Count
Biscuits		biscuits	0
Uncategorized		uncategorized	1

Adding a Post to a Category

When you are creating a Post as explained on page 48, you will notice that the category you have created will now appear down the right-hand side.

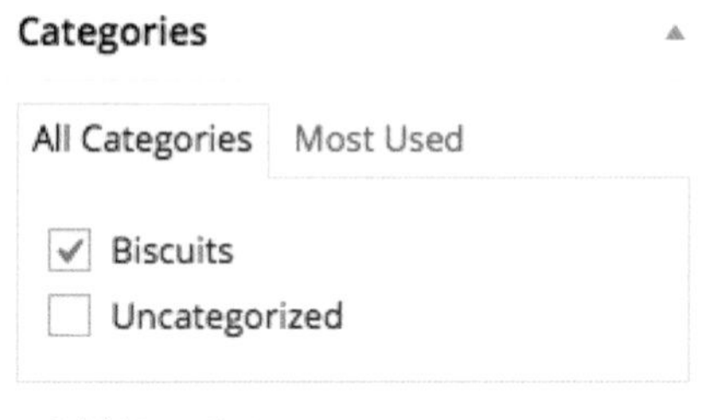

All you need to do is tick the box, and that post will appear under that particular category. This is really important when it comes to structuring your website.

You can also add categories right there in the post, by clicking **+Add New Category** inside the categories box.

Sliders

Homepage sliders can give a professional look to your website, and it isn't complicated. The one important thing to make sure of, is that your images are the correct size so they are not blurry. The size, of course, depends on the slider and your page set up. There are plenty of WordPress slider plugins to help you create the look you want. Soliloquy Lite is probably the best slider plugin out there. There is a free lite version and several paid options.

Sliders are usually found at the top of the homepage, and they come in various sizes. They use a slideshow style format, and use a mixture of different types of media.

1. From the Dashboard click **Plugins** > **Add New**
2. Search for Soliloquy Lite and click **Search Plugins**

3. Click **Install Now** and Activate the plugin

You will notice **Soliloquy** will have appeared in your Dashboard links

4. Click **Add New** under Soliloquy to begin building your slider

Add New Soliloquy Slider

Slider Title

5. Start by adding a title to the first text box, as shown above. This will not be shown on the slider itself

...cont'd

The default dimensions for Soliloquy sliders is 960 x 300 pixels. You can change this in the Slider Config which is explained on pages 65-66. Try to make sure the slider dimensions and image sizes are the same.

6 Next, start adding images to the slider. Select **Select Images** or just drop images in the center

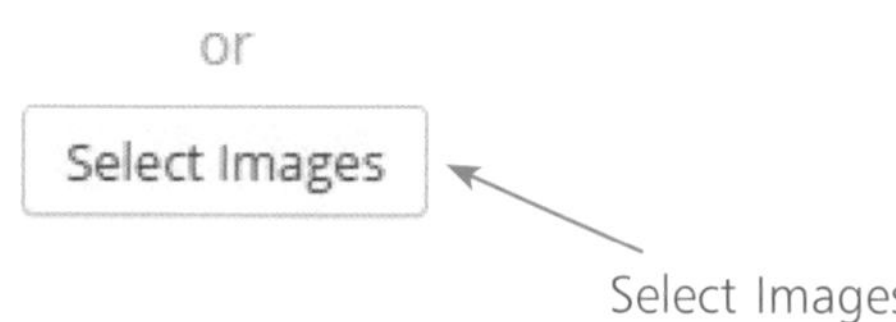

Select Images

7 Upload photos as shown in Chapter Four. Once you have chosen the images, they will appear at the bottom, ready to publish

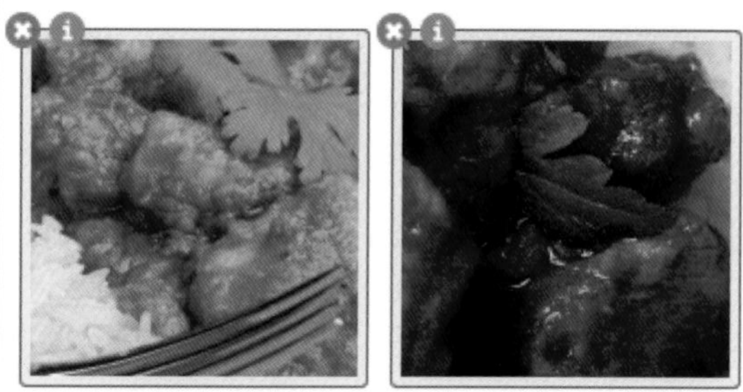

8 Click **Publish** which gets your slider ready for the website

9 When you click **Publish,** the shortcode should pop up as shown below. If it does not come up, then you can also access your shortcode from the main Soliloquy menu by clicking **Soliloquy** from the Dashboard

You can place this slider anywhere into your posts, pages, custom post types or widgets by using one of the shortcode(s) below:

```
[soliloquy id="77"]
[soliloquy slug="slider-title"]
```

You can add as many slides as you want but try to keep the file sizes of the images low, so it doesn't affect website performance.

10 Now go to a post or a page and enter your shortcode in the Visual Editor

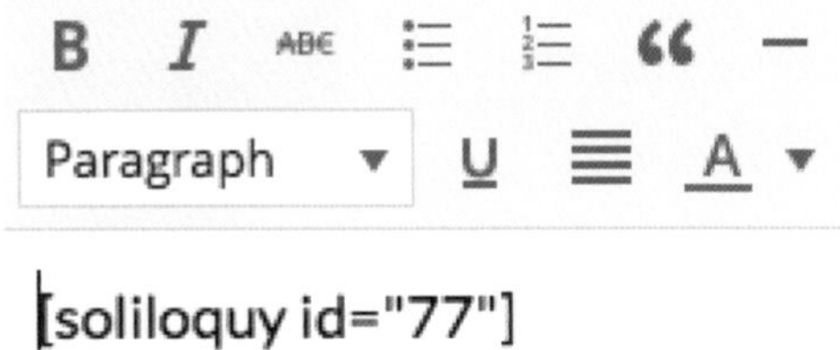

11 Click **Publish** or **Update**

Update

12 Now, if you visit your page, you will see that your slider appears

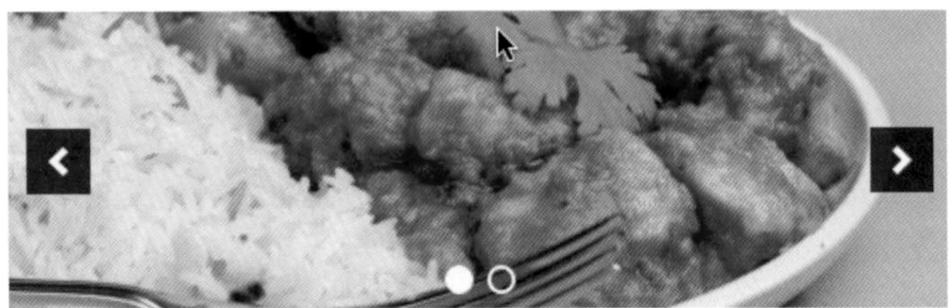

13 Next, you need to add text to your slider. Go to **Soliloquy** on the Dashboard and select your slider from the list

...cont'd

14 This time you need to click the small **"i"** icon next to one of the images

15 You will now be presented with a form to fill out, which looks similar to the one below

Image Title Nice Curry
Sets the image title attribute for the image.

Image Alt Text curry1
The image alt text is used for SEO. You should probc

Image Hyperlink http://www.thewebday.com
The image hyperlink determines what opens once tl

Open Link in New Tab? *If checked, the image hyperlink will open in a new tc*

Image Caption b i link ul ol li close tags
A delicious treat.

Try to keep your slider text short and sweet. All you need is just enough information to encourage the viewer to visit that particular page.

Image Title: Give a title for your image.

Image Alt Text: This is what will display if the image fails to load.

Image Hyperlink: You need to insert a link – this is where the user will go if they click the slide.

Open Link in New Tab?: If you want the link to open in a new browser tab then tick this box.

Image Caption: This is where you get to enter some text for this particular slide.

16. Remember to click **Save Metadata**. You will need to make sure you repeat the process for each slide

    Visit your live website and check out how your slider looks. Since you have already added the shortcode, you won't need to do it again

You can also add the PHP code to your theme files using the editor if you want to, as we discussed on page 42.

```
if ( function_exists(
'soliloquy' ) ) {
soliloquy( '77' ); }
```

Soliloquy Slider Settings

There are various settings you can change, which allow you to style the slider the way you want – without programming. To access the settings for your particular slider:

1. Go to **Soliloquy** from the Dashboard and select your slider from the list

   Slider Title   [soliloquy id="77"]

2. Select the **Config** option from the menu at the top

   Soliloquy Settings

...cont'd

Below are some of the various settings you can change:

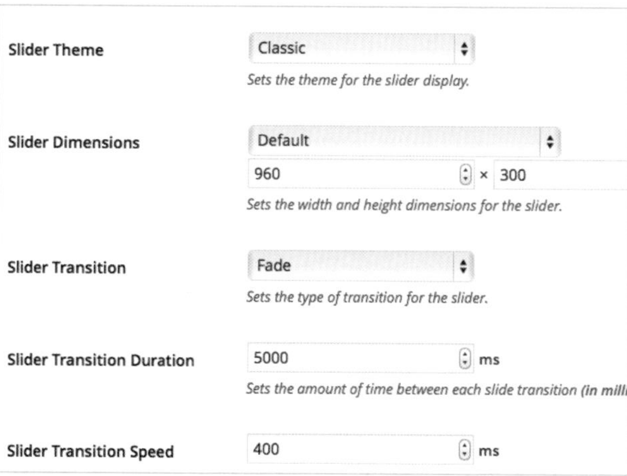

Slider Theme: Here you can choose from two particular themes, these are Base & Classic.

Slider Dimensions: Here you can set the height and width.

Slider Transition: You can choose the transition type for your slides. These include fade, scroll horizontal and scroll vertical.

Slider Transition Speed: This is the length of time it takes to go from one slide to another (in milliseconds).

Other settings include:

Slider Position: Set the position of the slider on the page.

Mobile Dimensions: Soliloquy is a fantastic choice when it comes to a slider for all devices. Here you can select the mobile dimension.

Autostart Slider?: If left ticked, then the slider will automatically start when the page is loaded. However, if you leave it unticked then the user will have to manually progress through the slides.

Pause on Hover?: This is unticked by default. However, the option is there if you want the slider to pause when the user hovers the mouse over it.

Loop Slider?: Ticking this box will loop the slider continuously. If left unticked then it will stop at the end of the slides.

5 Plugins

This chapter will introduce you to plugins. You will learn how to find, install, update, and even edit plugins.

Finding & Installing

Plugins are a great way to expand the functionality of your WordPress website. There are literally thousands available, and your options are limitless, which is another reason why WordPress is one of the leading platforms for Web Development.

There are many reasons why you may look for a plugin. For example, you may want a plugin so that you can turn your website into an eCommerce website, or you may want a plugin so that you can create a contact form for your website. There are loads of free ones available and also ones that come at a cost. We will start by looking for plugins within WordPress itself.

1. Click **Plugins** > **Add New** in the Dashboard

2. You will be presented with a search box, which allows you to search for terms relevant to the kind of plugin you are looking for. For example, if you are looking for a plugin that can set up contact forms, type "contact form" and click search

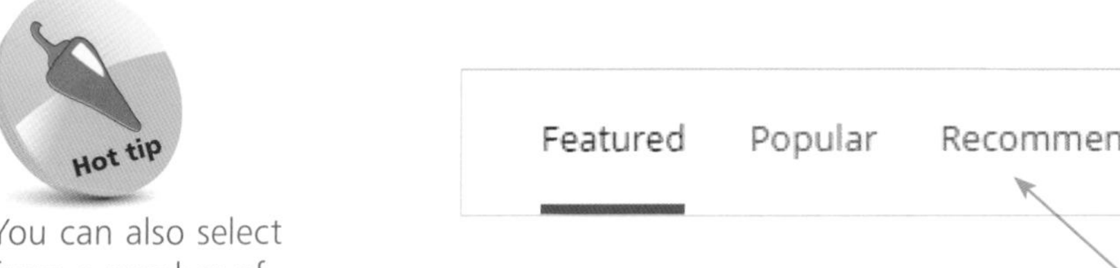

You can also select from a number of tags just below the search bar.

If you just want to look for the current featured plugins, most popular or newest, then you can choose from one of those categories at the top.

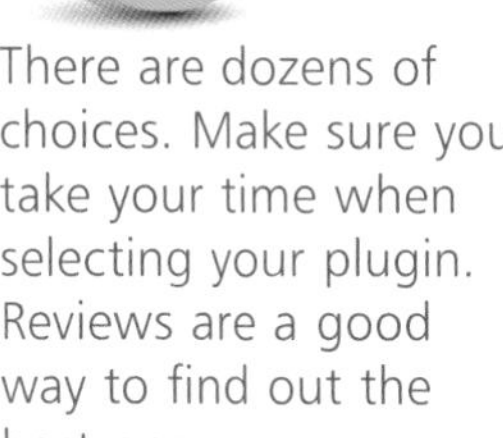

There are dozens of choices. Make sure you take your time when selecting your plugin. Reviews are a good way to find out the best ones.

3. After searching for "contact form" you will then be presented with a number of search results relevant to contact forms. Most plugins will have some kind of rating – this is the best way to judge which one will be best for your website. You can find out more details about each individual plugin by clicking **More Details**

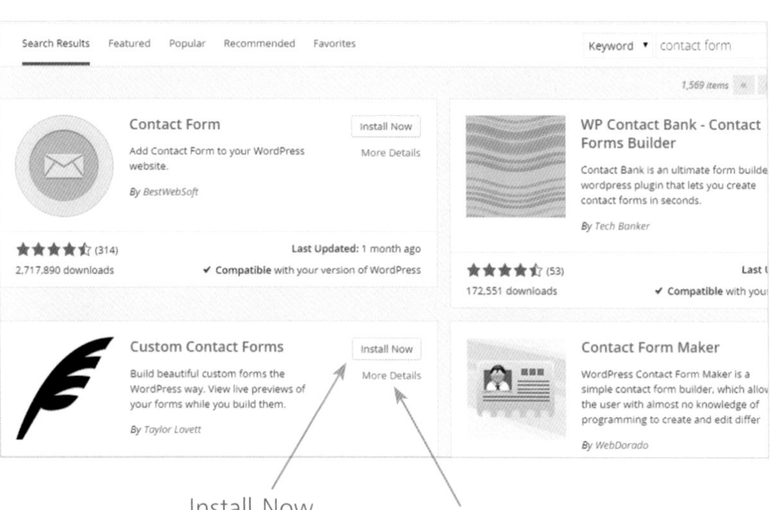

This will bring up a pop up with more information on the plugin, along with installation details and screenshots.

4. Read the installation steps carefully for that particular plugin. It will also be helpful to make a note of the author's website as it is likely that further documentation will be available there

5. Make sure you take a look at the reviews, and when the plugin was last updated. The more support you can get for the plugin, the better. You ideally want to choose one that has regular updates, especially since WordPress has a lot of updates

...cont'd

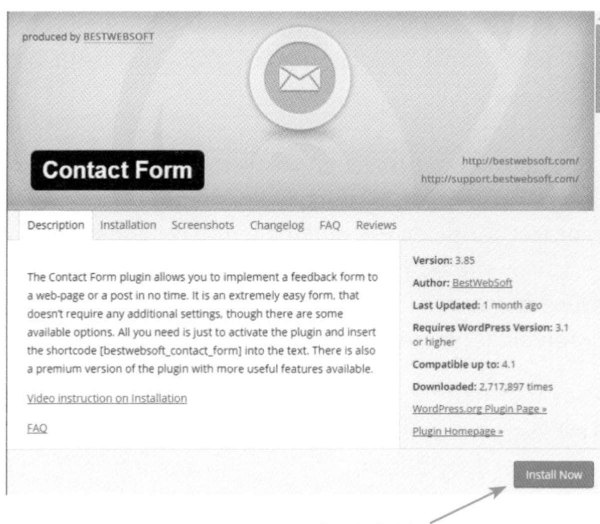

6. Once you are happy with your choice, click **Install Now** either from the pop up window, or from the search result window

7. Once installed, it should give you the option to activate the plugin there and then

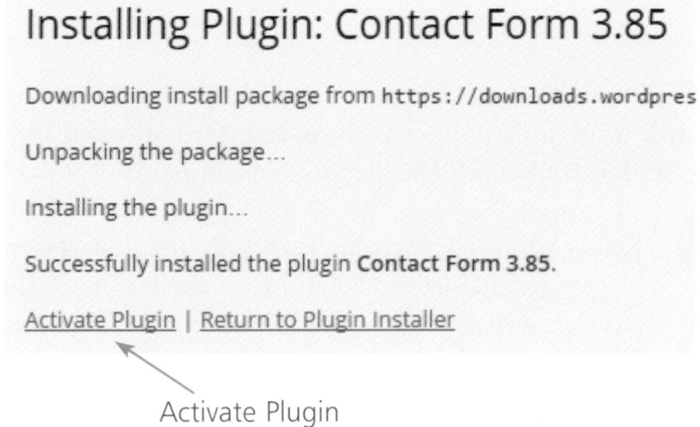

8. If you miss the screen then you can easily go to **Plugins > Installed Plugins.** Scroll down until you find the plugin. and select **Activate** just underneath the title

After this point, each plugin will have its own unique setup. Some will require you to configure some settings right from the start. Generally you can find these settings by going to your **Installed Plugins** page, scrolling down to your plugin and selecting **Settings** under the plugin.

If not, your installed plugin will appear somewhere on the Dashboard, usually on the menu down the left hand side or under Settings.

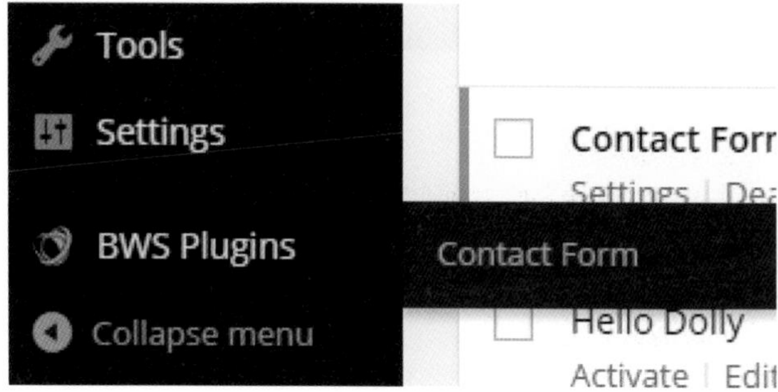

Finding Plugin Documentation

Remember each individual plugin setup will be different once it is installed. This makes it extremely important for you to read the documentation. To find the documentation for your plugin:

1. Select **Plugins** > **Installed Plugins** from the Dashboard
2. Select **View Details** on the chosen plugin
3. Select the **Installation** link. Most developers use this area to provide steps on how to use it, or give a link to an external website for full documentation

Description | Installation | Screenshots | Changelog | FAQ | Reviews

Uploading a Plugin

You might find a really nice WordPress Plugin on an external website that you want to upload. Some developers will let you try a lite version of their plugin and then want you to upgrade to a pro version for more features. If you have downloaded or purchased from an external source then it is pretty easy to upload the plugin file (usually .zip).

Make sure you are buying plugins from a trusted source. You should do your research before purchasing by finding reviews for the plugin or by finding out more about the developer.

1. Click **Plugins** > **Add New** in the Dashboard

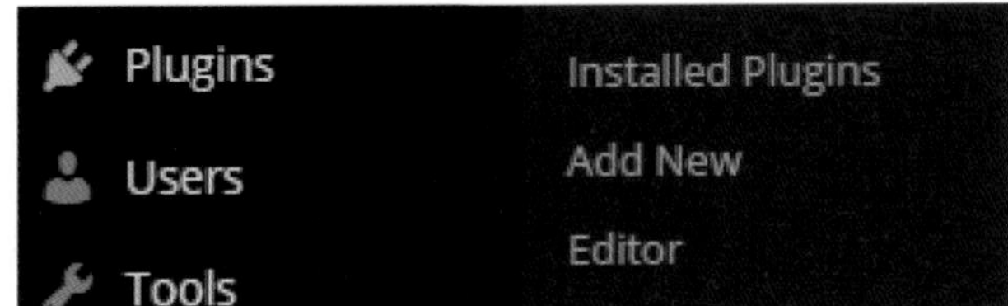

2. Select **Upload Plugin**

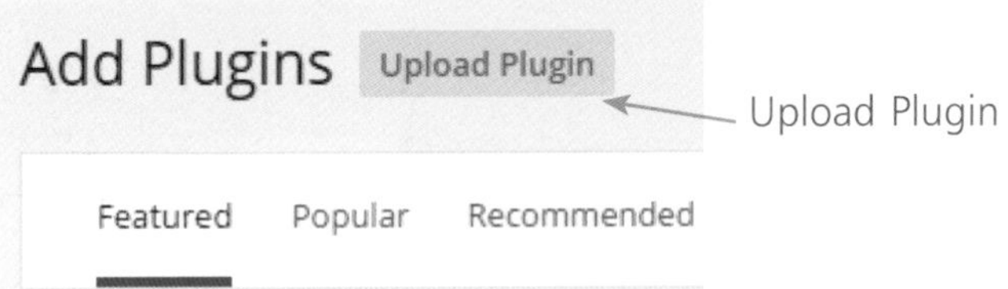

3. You will now be asked for the plugin in .zip format. When you purchased or downloaded the file, you should have been given a zip file to upload. Select **Choose File** and then locate your plugin .zip file. Once you have found your file, click **Install Now**

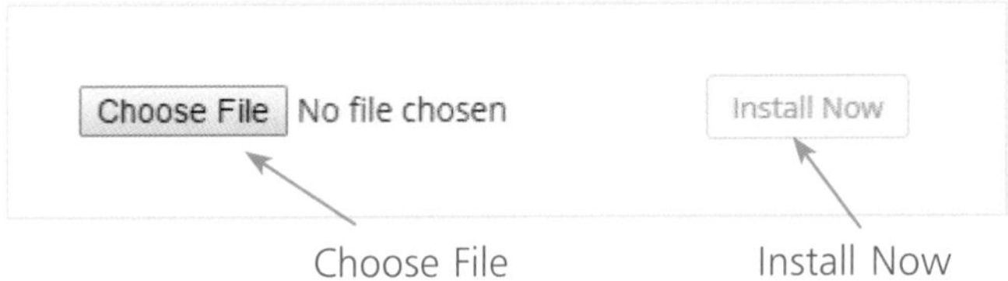

4. Once it has finished installing, you will still need to activate the plugin, like you did before when you selected a plugin from the search results (see page 70)

Installed Plugins

The **Installed Plugins** page is where you can view all your currently installed plugins, and you can also deactivate and delete them from here. Try to keep a note of all the plugins you install. Make sure you deactivate any you are not using, as it can slow down your website or cause conflicts with others. The bigger your site gets, the more plugins you are likely to use. To access the Installed Plugins page:

Select **Plugins** > **Installed Plugins**

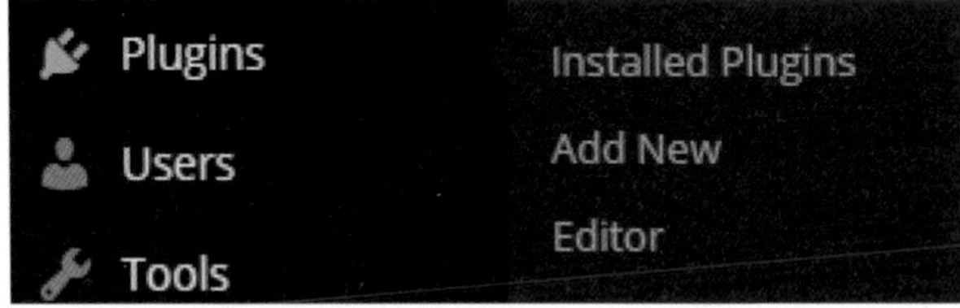

Deactivating a Plugin

To deactivate a plugin, find the appropriate plugin and select **Deactivate**.

Deleting a Plugin

To delete a plugin, find the appropriate plugin and select **Delete**. You will need to deactivate the plugin before you have the option to delete.

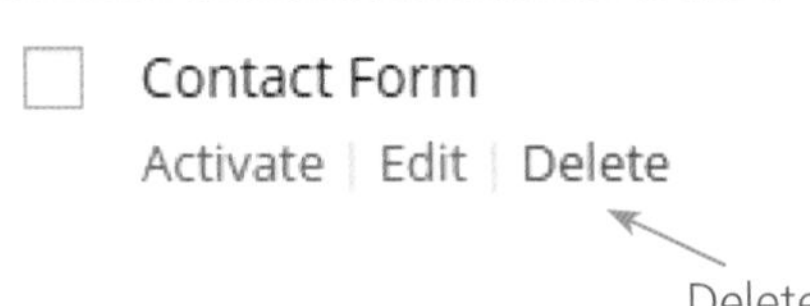

This page will also give you the chance to visit the website for each particular plugin. All you need to do is click **Visit plugin site** under that particular plugin.

Try to deactivate and delete any plugins you are not using, so that there are no conflictions. Having too many plugins may slow your website down.

Updating Plugins

Now and again you will need to update your plugins. Developers will constantly make improvements to their plugins, so that your website can function effectively.

The Signs

You will know when a plugin needs to be updated when a a number appears next to Plugins on the Dashboard.

For example, if there is a 1 next to Plugins, then it means 1 plugin need to be updated.

1. Click on **Plugins** > **Installed Plugins**
2. Now, select **Updates Available** along the top

Updates Available

Plugins Add New

All (31) | Active (18) | Inactive (13) | Update Available (11)

Bulk Actions ▾ Apply

Plugin Description

Akismet
Settings | Deactivate | Edit

Used by millions, Akismet is quite possibly the best way in t protected from spam even while you sleep. To get started: key, and 3) Go to your Akismet configuration page, and sav

Version 3.0.2 | By Automattic | Visit plugin site

There is a new version of Akismet available. View version 3.0.4 details or update now.

3. Now, select the tick box next to the plugin and select **Update** from the dropdown box and click **Apply**, and this will update the plugin

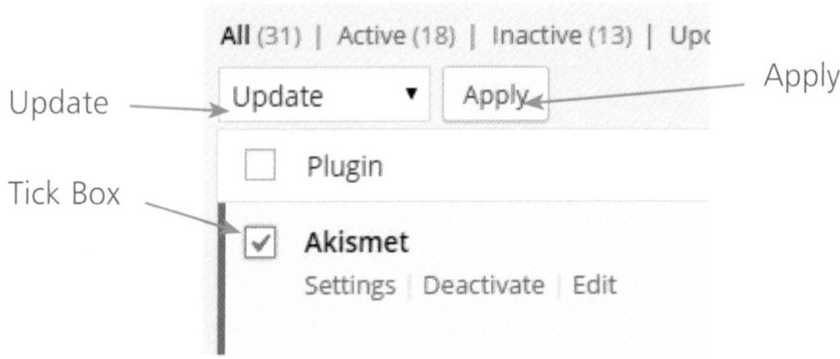

Must-have Plugins

There are lots of great Plugins out there to get you started and many are being developed every day, so you will never be short of ways to boost the functionality of your website. Here are some of the best ones out there:

WooCommerce

We will be having a look at this plugin in more detail in Chapter Six. This plugin is FREE and allows you to build an online shop for your website. This is very handy if you are planning to sell your products online to customers.

Contact Forms 7

All websites need a contact form, so that customers and readers can get in touch with you. This plugin makes it very easy to set one up.

WordPress SEO by Yoast

This is a great plugin that optimizes your WordPress blog/website for SEO (Search Engine Optimization). SEO has become vital for ranking on search engines, so this plugin will really help you maxmize your website's potential (see pages 106-110).

bbPress

If you are looking to set up a forum for your website, then look no further. This does all the hard work for you. It is very simple to set up and has become the top choice for setting up forums on WordPress websites (see pages 123-128).

Akismet

This is a good one, if your website or blog is going to have user interaction. It checks comments on your website to see if they look like spam.

Google XML Sitemaps

Sitemaps will help index your website better with search engines. This plugin is great for generating an XML sitemap (see page 157) for your website.

Plugins Editor

Do not edit code unless you have a good knowledge of PHP.

Just like with themes, you are able to edit the plugins if you have knowledge of PHP. There might be a functionality you want to extend or edit inside WordPress or maybe add a feature that was not included in the original plugin. To edit plugins:

1. Click **Plugins** > **Editor** in the Dashboard

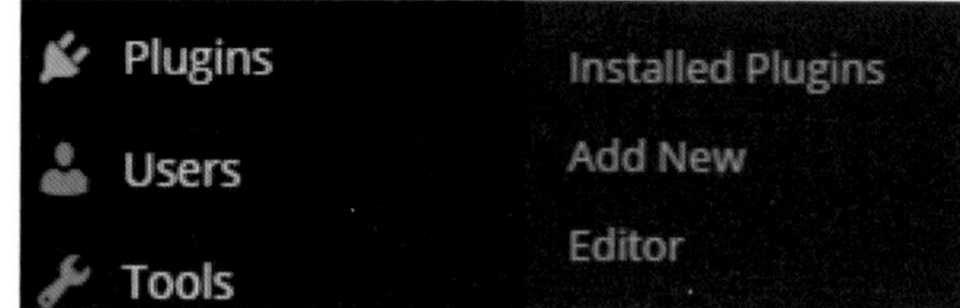

2. Select the plugin you want to edit from the dropdown on the right hand side

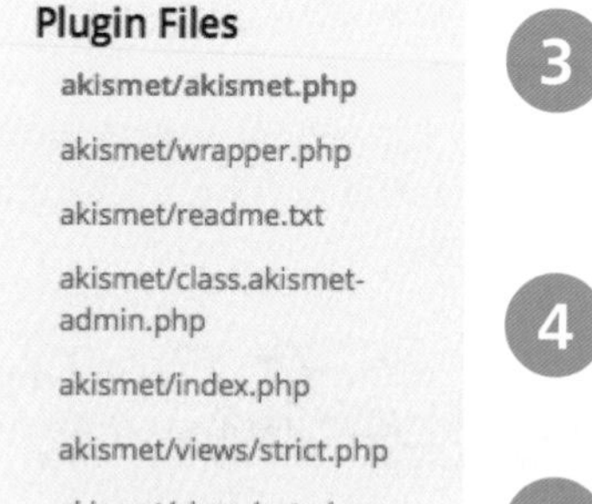

3. From the list of files on the right hand side, select the one you want to edit

4. Make the changes in the code window

5. Click **Update File** when you are finished

Make sure you keep backups of files in case something goes wrong.

Editing **akismet/akismet.php** (inactive)

```
}

define( 'AKISMET_VERSION', '3.0.1' );
define( 'AKISMET__MINIMUM_WP_VERSION', '3.1' );
define( 'AKISMET__PLUGIN_URL', plugin_dir_url( __FILE__ ) );
define( 'AKISMET__PLUGIN_DIR', plugin_dir_path( __FILE__ ) );
define( 'AKISMET_DELETE_LIMIT', 100000 );

register_activation_hook( __FILE__, array( 'Akismet', 'plugin_activation' ) );
register_deactivation_hook( __FILE__, array( 'Akismet', 'plugin_deactivation' ) );

require_once( AKISMET__PLUGIN_DIR . 'class.akismet.php' );
require_once( AKISMET__PLUGIN_DIR . 'class.akismet-widget.php' );
```

Code Window

6 Creating an Online Store

This chapter will introduce you to a plugin called WooCommerce, which will allow you to build your own online store with WordPress.

WooCommerce Setup

You might think that creating an online store is difficult. However, WordPress makes it very easy. Now that you have a better grasp of WordPress, let's have a look at how you can build your online store with ease.

It will be handy to have a payment method set up. If you already have a PayPal account then you are good to go!

Installing WooCommerce

WooCommerce is a free but very powerful plugin that allows you to set up a shop and easily configure it using the WordPress Dashboard. To install WooCommerce:

1. Navigate to **Plugins** in the WordPress Dashboard
2. Now, click **Add New**
3. In the search box type **WooCommerce** and click Search Plugins. It should appear as the first search result

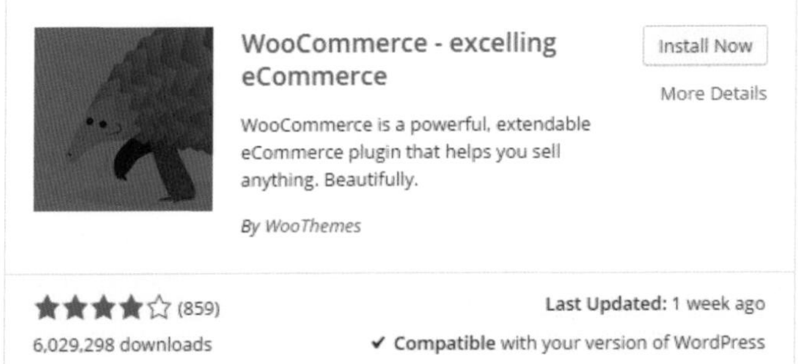

4. Click **Install Now** to install the plugin

Activate Plugin

5. Click **Activate Plugin** and WooCommerce is all ready to go!

WooCommerce should now appear in your WordPress Dashboard as shown above.

...cont'd

Now that WooCommerce has been installed, you will probably notice in your Dashboard somewhere near the top that WooCommerce has brought an alert to your attention. It will ask you to install WooCommerce pages as shown below.

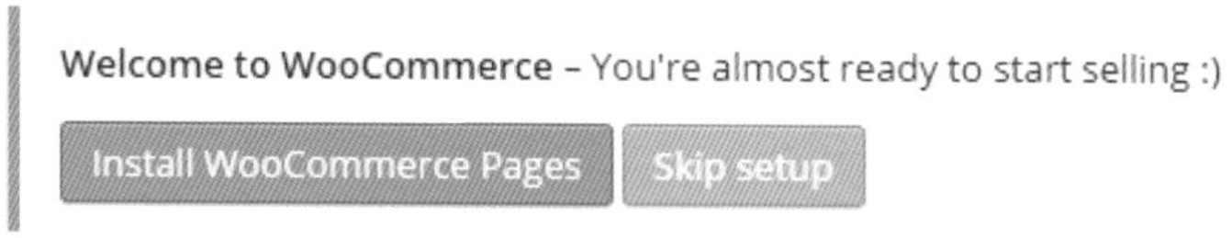

Welcome to WooCommerce – You're almost ready to start selling :)

Install WooCommerce Pages | Skip setup

1. Click **Install WooCommerce Pages**

2. If you now head to your WordPress website, you will notice that several links have been added to the website:

- **Cart** – This will eventually display everything that the user has added to their shopping cart.
- **Checkout** – This is where the user will go to start the process of buying the products they want.
- **My Account** – This is where the user can change their buying or account details, billing address etc.
- **Shop** – This page will display all the products you have for sale.

These are the basic pages needed to get your online shop off the ground. If you check out the Shop page, you will find there are currently no products for sale as you haven't added any yet.

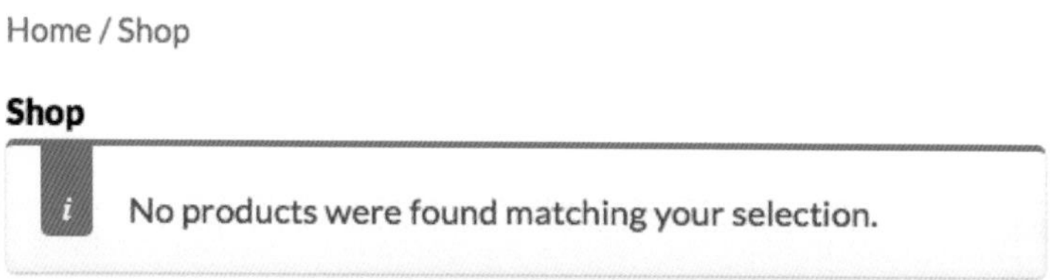

Home / Shop

Shop

No products were found matching your selection.

By the end of this chapter, you will have your own online store up and running.

Adding Products

There can be no shop without products so let's begin by showing you how to adding a product to the store.

1. Select **Products** from your WordPress Dashboard. It should be right underneath WooCommerce. You will now be presented with a page that looks very similar to what you see with posts and pages

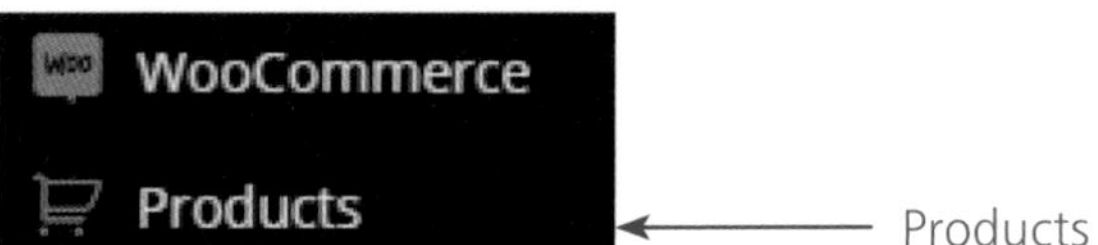

2. Click **Add Product** from the top of the page. You will notice that this is very similar to adding any post or page

Add Product

3. Add the item title and the item description as shown below

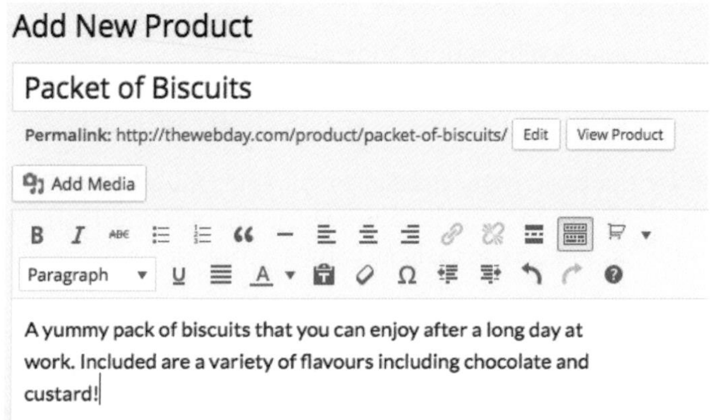

4. You will notice on the right hand side that you can create a product category. In the example above, a packet of biscuits would fit well in a "Foods" category. Click **+ Add New Product Category** and then type in "Foods" as show in the screenshot on the next page. Your product will now automatically be part of the Foods category

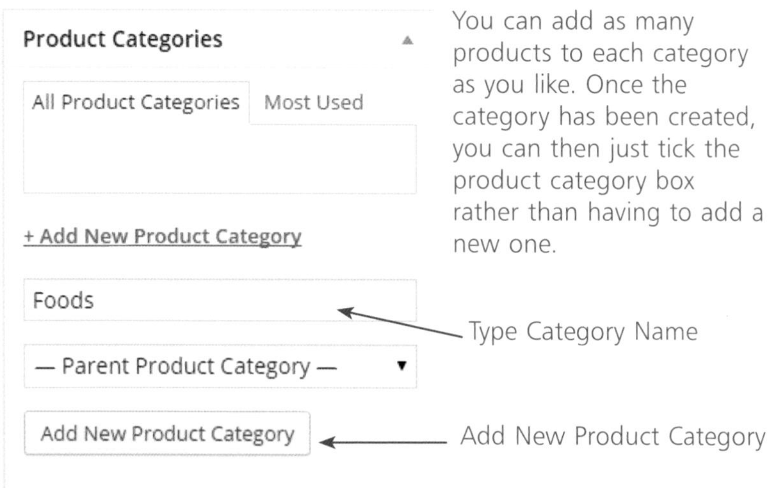

You can add as many products to each category as you like. Once the category has been created, you can then just tick the product category box rather than having to add a new one.

Try to keep your products in relevant categories, so that the customer can easily find items.

5. Scroll down to the Product Data section where you need to add in more information about your product

You will see a dropdown box. Choose **Simple Product**, for this example, and complete the sections as follows:

Virtual TickBox: Check this if your item is a virtual item.
Downloadable Tickbox: If your item is a downloadable item like an ebook, then this would be appropriate.
SKU: This is your own identification code for the product (Stock Keeping Unit).
Regular Price: This is the standard price for the item.
Sale Price: If the item is on sale, then you would put the sale price here.

We will cover the advanced product options later in the book (see pages 90-94).

Add Product Image

The last thing to do is add a product image so that the customer can see what they are buying.

1. On the right, you will see a box that says **Featured Image**. Select **Set featured image**

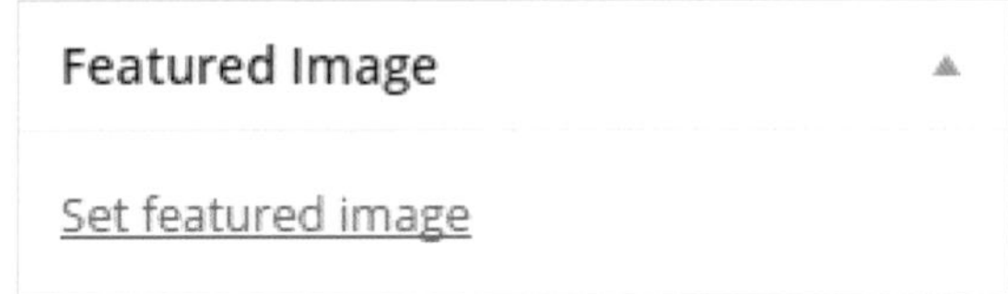

2. Upload your product image or select from the Media Library, just like you did in Chapter Four

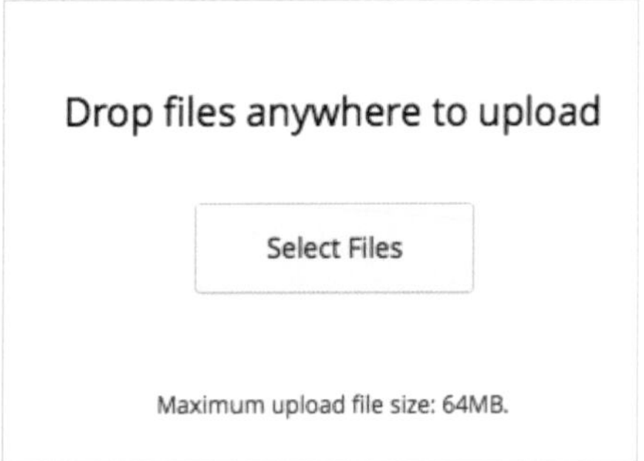

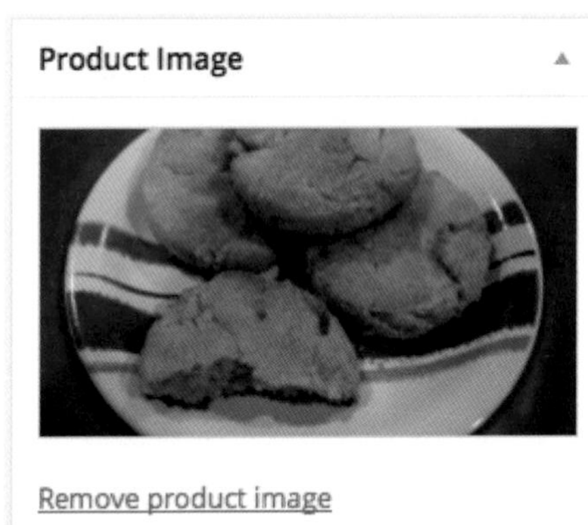

3. Select **Set Product Image**

Set product image

4. Click **Publish** at the top right of your page to update your product

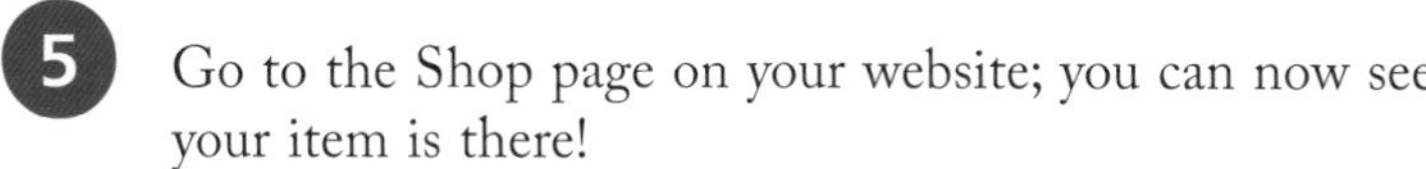

5. Go to the Shop page on your website; you can now see your item is there!

Packet of Biscuits

£9.99

ADD TO CART

You will notice that the image is showing, along with the title and price and the **Add to Cart** button has automatically been added so that users can purchase straight away!

6. If you click on the title, you will be sent through to the product page where it also shows the description along with the same **Add to Cart** option

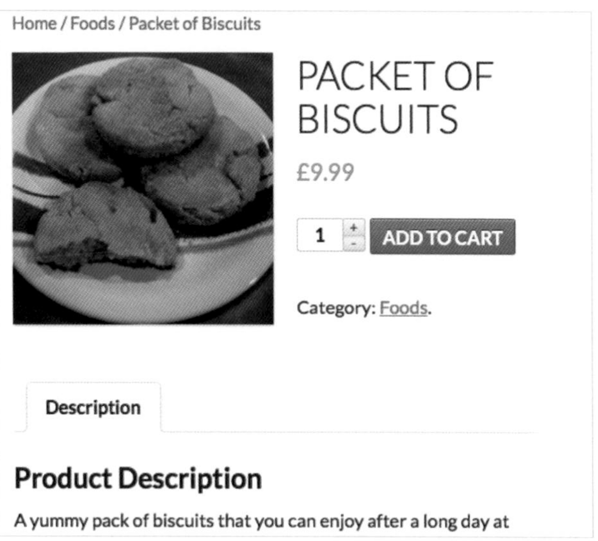

7. You can now go ahead and add more products to your store – there is no limit to the numer of products you can add. Every time you add a product, it will automatically appear in the shop page

Checkout

Now that you have products set up, you need to set up the checkout so that customers can pay for their items. There are plenty of payment methods that you can use like Bank Transfer, Cheque, Paypal etc. To begin the checkout process:

1. Select **WooCommerce** > **Settings**

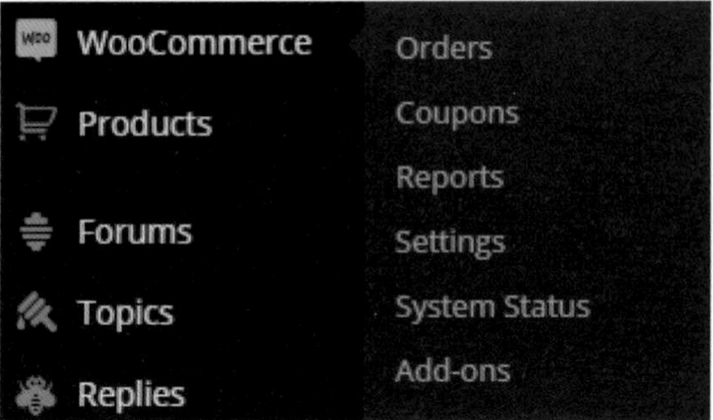

2. Select **Checkout** from the options along the top

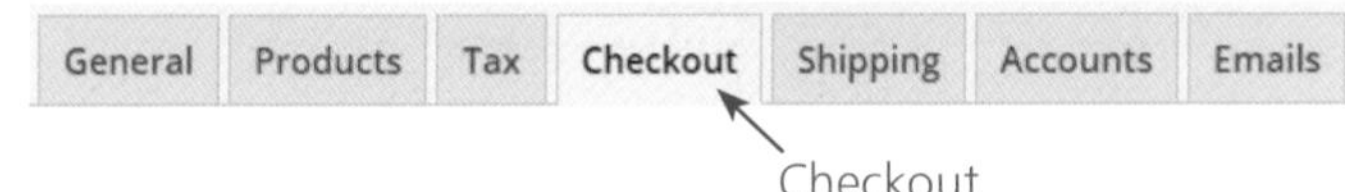

Checkout Options

- **Coupons:** Toggle the box to allow the use of coupons on your website.
- **Checkout:** Toggle the use of guest checkout (for users who don't have an account).
- **Checkout Pages:** Here you can select which WordPress pages you want to use for each WooCommerce page. For example, you might want to set a Terms & Conditions page.
- **Checkout Endpoints:** Endpoints are appended to your page URLs to handle specific actions during the checkout process. For example, for order received, it might be "order-received". This would make your domain: **www.domain.com/order-received/**
- **Payment Gateways:** This is where you can set up various payment gateway settings like PayPal or Credit Card.

Set up PayPal

PayPal is a very popular choice with online customers, as it's safe and secure. Let's set up your checkout so that the customer can pay funds into your PayPal account during checkout.

Paypal is one of the most commonly used online payment methods. You will need to set up an account online at www.paypal.com

1. Click the **PayPal** link at the top under the Checkout menu. Or you can also select it by clicking the **Settings** button next to the PayPal option in the Payment Gateway area

2. The next page will present a lot of options. However, you will not need all of them. These are the main ones:

- **Enable/Disable PayPal Standard:** Make sure that this tickbox is ticked so you are able to accept PayPal payments.
- **Title:** This is how you want the option to be displayed on the website.
- **Description:** This will control the description that the user sees during checkout.
- **PayPal Email:** This is the email address you use for your PayPal account. You need this to receive payments.

3. Once you are finished, click **Save Changes**. The buyer can now select PayPal at checkout!

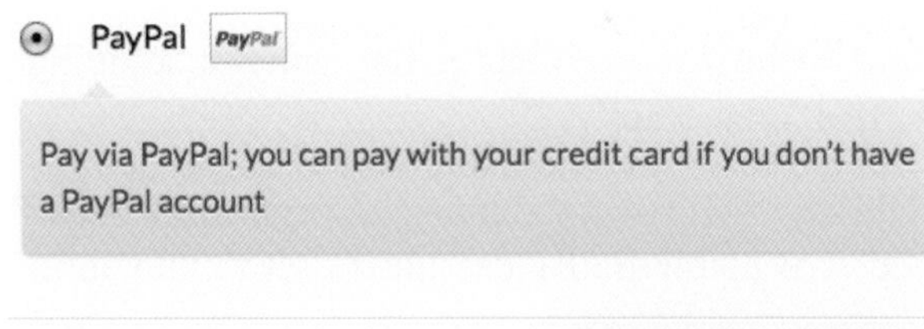

Shipping

Another important part of owning an online store is the shipping process. WooCommerce has handled this well, and it is not too complicated.

1. Select **WooCommerce > Orders**
2. Select **Shipping** from the top bar

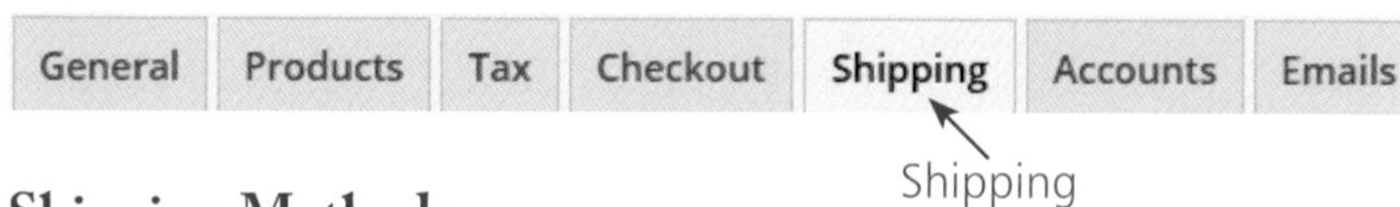

Shipping Methods

You will notice along the bottom, there are a number of shipping methods ready for setup. You will need to configure them yourself to get them right for your store. At first, **Free Shipping** will be the only one enabled. So we will now look at the settings for **Flat Rate**.

1. Select **Flat Rate** from the second menu under the top bar or click the **Settings** button next to **Flat Rate** under Shipping Methods

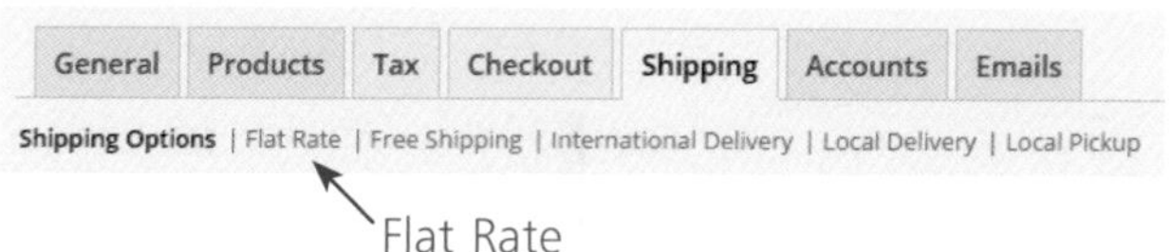

2. You are now faced with a number of settings you will need to configure to get this shipping method working

- **Enable/Disable:** First of all you need to tick this box to enable this method.
- **Method Title:** You can change the name to something else other than “Flat Rate”.
- **Availability:** You need to choose the countries your shipping method is available in. By default it’s set to all countries.
- **Tax Status:** You will need to choose whether or not the shipping method is taxable or not.

- **Cost Per Order:** Here is where you can enter the cost for this method per order.
- **Additional Rates:** This can get a little complicated. Bear in mind the next few fields are not mandatory.
  This section lets you add a few additional rates to the exisiting method. First of all the format looks like this:
  Option Name | Additional Cost | Per-cost type (order, class or item)

Option Name | Additional Cost [+- Percents%] | Per Cost Type (order, class, or item)

For example, if you entered £7.00 for **Cost Per Order**, and you had entered the following in the Additional Rates box:

Express | 5 | order

Then the following two options would be available to the customer.

Flat Rate: £7.00 (Standard Cost Per Order)
Express: £12.00 (Standard Cost Per Order + Extra £5)

- **Additional Costs:** There is also a table right at the bottom, where you can define any additional costs. Remember that these will be added to all flat rates. You can define these based on shipping, cost and handling fee.
- **Minimum Handling Fee:** This is to set a minimum handling fee for your shipping class. When working with percentages this can come in extremely handy.

3. When you have finished, you can click **Save Changes**

Viewing Orders

Once you get the orders coming in, you need to know how to view them and sort through them efficiently. WooCommerce offers a dedicated section to manage your orders easily.

Select **WooCommerce > Orders**

You will now see a page that displays all your current orders. You will see in the example below there is just one order there.

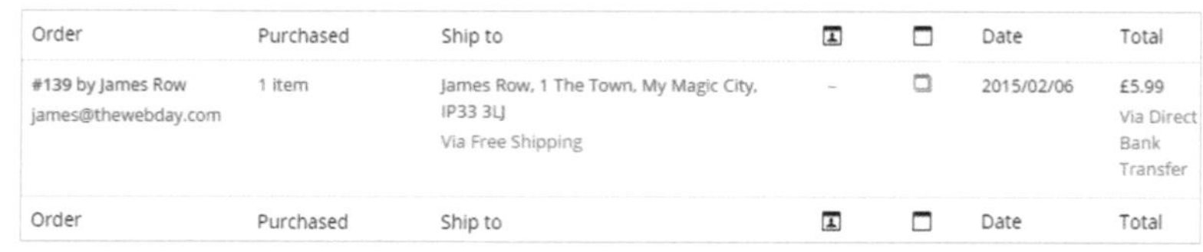

Order	Purchased	Ship to			Date	Total
#139 by James Row james@thewebday.com	1 item	James Row, 1 The Town, My Magic City, IP33 3LJ Via Free Shipping	–		2015/02/06	£5.99 Via Direct Bank Transfer
Order	Purchased	Ship to			Date	Total

You can filter your orders by using the links at the top of the order section.

2 If you click on the order number, you will see a more detailed breakdown of the order

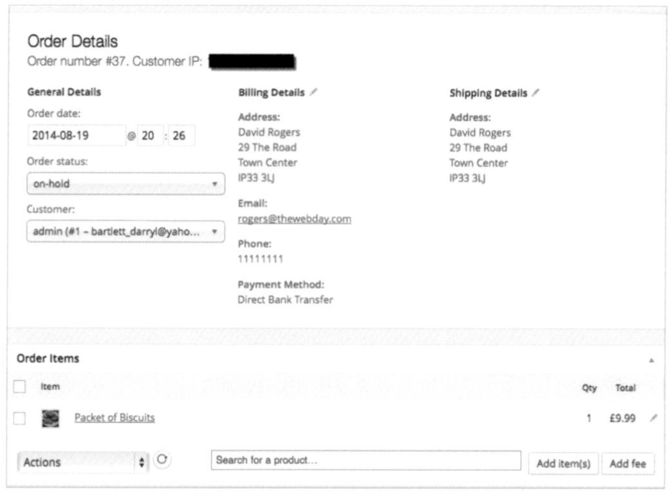

Order Details

At the top you will see your order status, and it will display order date, billing address, shipping address details and of course payment method. You can edit the address too.

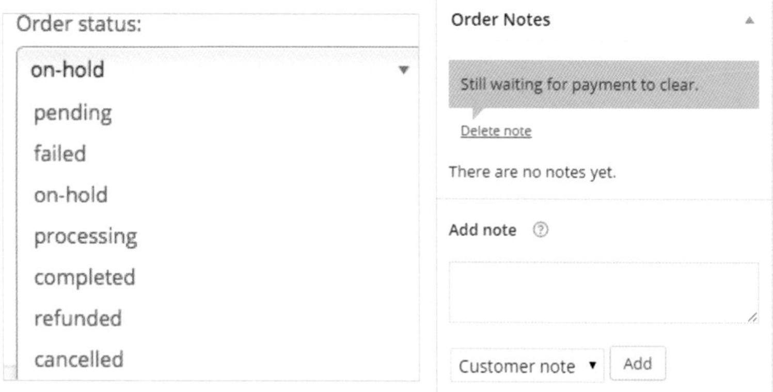

You will also notice the Order Notes box, which will make automated notes based on the order. You can, however, add your own if you need to.

If your product is a downloadable product, then you can grant access at the bottom by typing in the name of the product and clicking **Grant Access**.

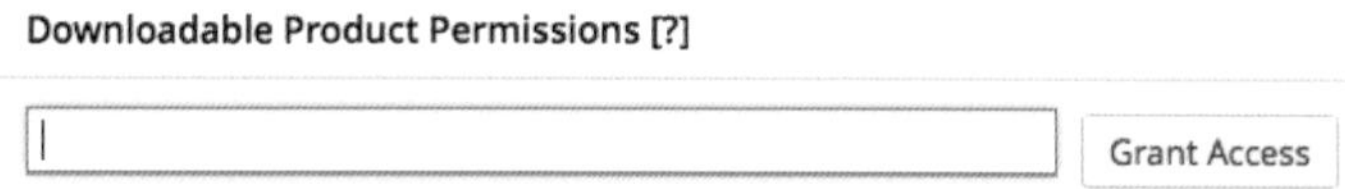

Manual Order

If you want to add a manual order from within WordPress then it's pretty simple to do.

1. Select **WooCommerce** > **Orders**
2. Select **Add Order** from the top

   Orders Add Order

3. A new form is presented for you to fill out. Of course this is a longer process and requires you to fill out everything

Use a plugin called **WooCommerce Print Invoice & Delivery Note** if you want to print order invoices and delivery notes. Just search for it in the WordPress Dashboard and install and activate the plugin.

Advanced Product Options

Let’s go through some of the advanced options you can set when creating a product.

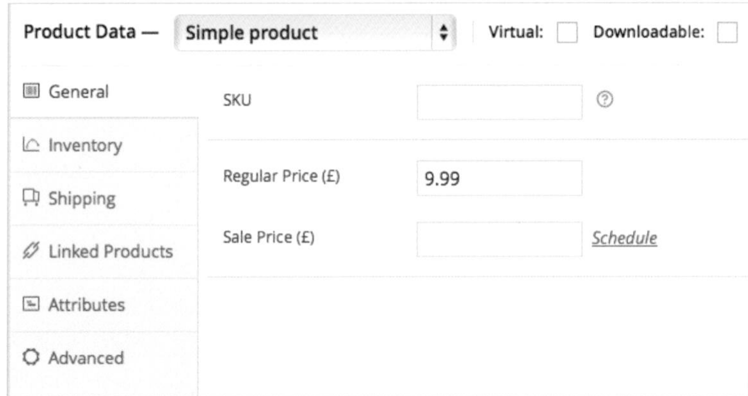

In the example shown on pages 80-83 the General options were already set when you added the price, but let’s look through some of the other options.

Inventory

Manage stock?	☑ *Enable stock management at product level*
Stock Qty	0
Allow Backorders?	Do not allow
Stock status	In stock
Sold Individually	☐ *Enable this to only allow one of this item to be bought in a single order*

Manage Stock: If you tick this box, it will allow you to set a quantity of how many of the item you have in stock. It will then continue to keep an accurate count of the stock left.
Stock Quantity: Here you will enter how many of that item you have in stock.
Allow Backorders: When the item is out of stock, you need to let the system know if you will continue to take orders for that item.
Stock Status: You can select whether or not the item is currently in stock.

Sold Individually: If this is selected, then the customer can only buy one of these in a single order.

Shipping

This section will allow you to set dimensions and weight for a particular item. You can also assign a shipping class to it.

Linked Products

Up-Sells: Here you can add items that you want to recommend to the customer rather than the currently viewed item. For example, the customer may be viewing a standard wallet, and you want to recommend a leather one to them.
Cross-Sells: Here you can add other products that you might recommend to the customer based on their current order.
Grouping: You may want to set your product as part of a grouped product.

Advanced

Purchase Note: Here you can enter a note, which will be sent to the customer after they purchase that particular item.
Menu Order: This is the position you want your item to appear in. For example, the items will appear numerically 1, 2, 3, 4 etc.
Enable Reviews: Ticking this box will enable customers to leave reviews for the product.

Setting up a Variable Item

The options above will give your simple products extra detail, but let's say you are selling t-shirts in multiple colors or sizes. This is where Variable Products comes in handy.

Firstly you need to change the item from a Simple Product to a Variable Product. You can start by creating a new product and then selecting **Variable Product** under the Product Data section

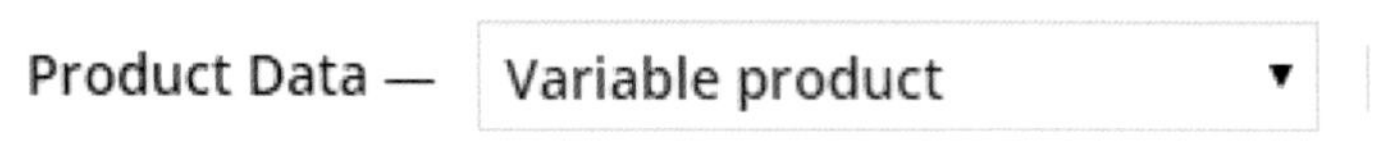

...cont'd

You can add as many variations as you like, which allows you to add several different options for your customers.

2. Select the **Attributes** tab. This will allow you to create separate attributes for your product, like color or size

3. Click **Add** to bring up a new form

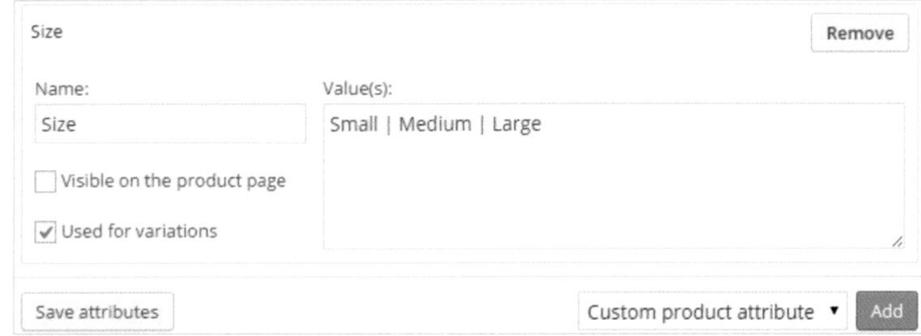

- **Name:** In this example, "Size" has been entered in this box, because you are setting up three sizes for the item.
- **Value(s):** Here you will put the sizes of your item. Each size needs to be separated by "|". For example, here you would put "Small | Medium | Large".
- **Used for variations:** It is important to click this, so that your variations are set up correctly for the next stage.

4. Click **Update** at the top of the page, or **Publish** if you created a new product

Update

5. Click the **Variations** tab, as your variations will now be ready to set up

6. Click **Add Variation** on the right hand side

7. Using the dropdown box on the left, select your variation type, for example **Small** and then enter your regular price

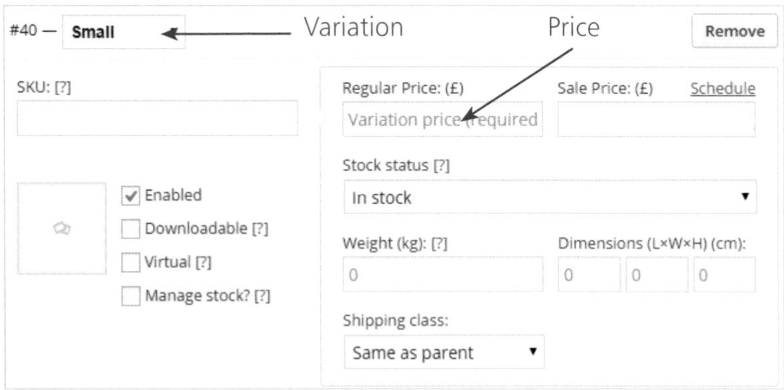

8. You can then repeat the process for the other two variations (Medium and Large), so that you have a price set up for each variation

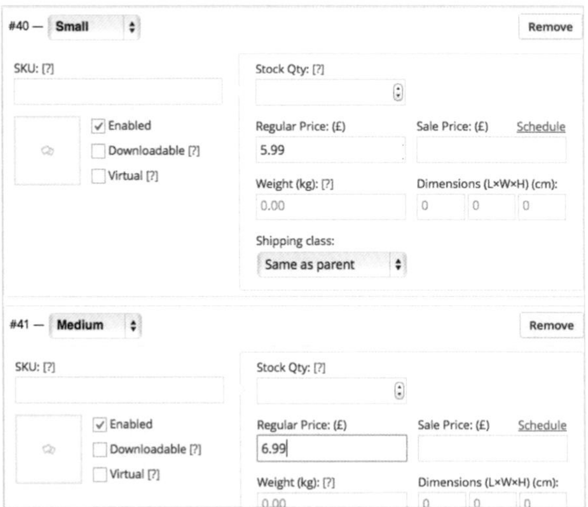

...cont'd

9. Once you have finished, remember to click **Update** to save your changes

You will now notice you can select from the three variations – Small, Medium and Large.

When your customer lands on the t-shirt page, you might want to have a default selection. To do this, you need to go back to your product page.

1. Click **Variation** in the product data

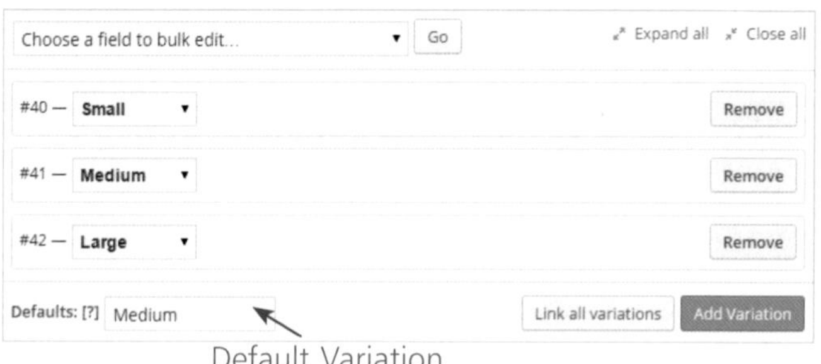

2. Select one of the variations from the Defaults dropdown box

You should now be on your way to creating your own online store. WooCommerce has a lot of add-ons to help you enhance your store even further!

7 Settings & Tools

This chapter explains the different Settings sections and will guide you through what each change will do. You will also learn more about the Tools section.

General Settings

We are now going to take a look at the Settings section of the WordPress Dashboard. This is where you will configure your WordPress website. Let's start by taking a look at the General section. Go to **Settings > General.**

The Settings section is probably the most important area of WordPress. It controls the basic foundations of your website.

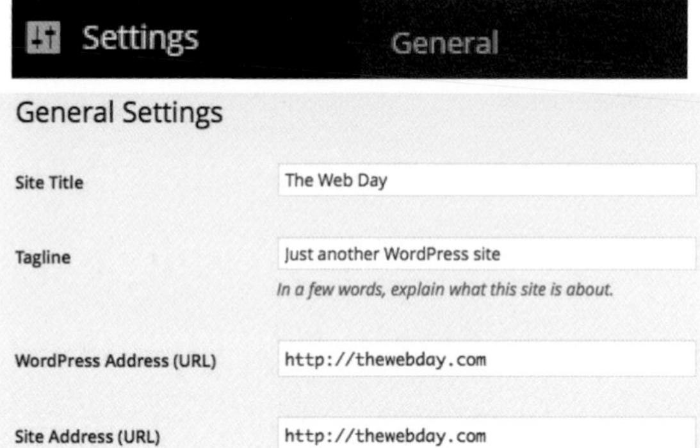

Site Title: This is basically the name for your website. Name it as you wish!

Tagline: This is used to explain what your website is about.

WordPress Address (URL): Don't worry too much about this one. This is most likely going to be the same as the Site Address. The WordPress URL is the location of your WordPress files.

Site Address (URL): This is the URL for your website homepage. As mentioned above, both WordPress and Site Address are very likely to be the same.

E-mail Address: This should contain the email address you entered when you installed WordPress. It is mainly used for user notifications or password reset.

Membership: Tick this box if you want anyone to be able to register for this website.

New User Default Role: If you ticked the Membership box, then this dropdown box defines the type of privileges that you want new users to have.

Timezone: Choose your current time zone.

Date Format: Choose how you want the date to display on your website.

Time Format: Choose how you want the time to display on your website.

Week Starts On: The default setting is Monday. However, you can select your preferred start date for WordPress calendars.

Writing Settings

The Writing Settings are used for posts, interface settings as well as things like post via email. You can access this by clicking **Settings > Writing.**

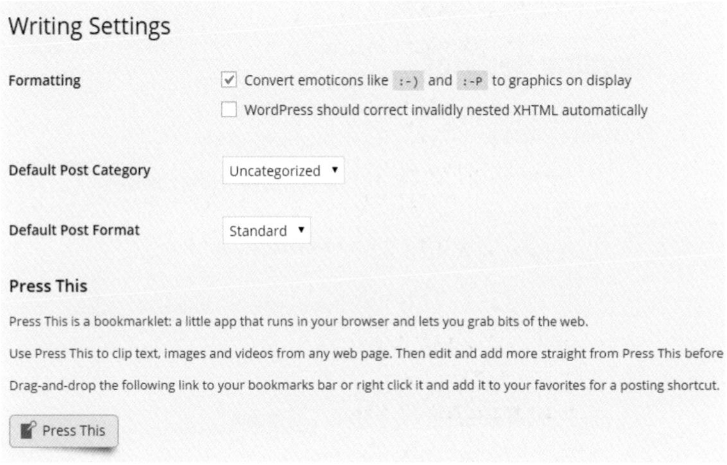

Writing Settings

Formatting
☑ Convert emoticons like :-) and :-P to graphics on display
☐ WordPress should correct invalidly nested XHTML automatically

Default Post Category: Uncategorized

Default Post Format: Standard

Press This

Press This is a bookmarklet: a little app that runs in your browser and lets you grab bits of the web.

Use Press This to clip text, images and videos from any web page. Then edit and add more straight from Press This before

Drag-and-drop the following link to your bookmarks bar or right click it and add it to your favorites for a posting shortcut.

Press This

Formatting: The first tick box (***Convert emoticons like :-) and :-P to graphics on display***) is automatically ticked by default. It converts emoticons to onscreen graphics. Emoticons are the ones we are used to using in text messages. The second tick box (***WordPress should correct invalidly nested XHTML automatically***) will basically check that what you are writing is valid XHTML code. This is most likely to be unticked by default.

Default Post Category: We talked about Post Categories on page 45. WordPress will automatically assign a post to this category if none is assigned.

Default Post Format: There are various different post formats that can be used depending on the theme. For example, a Standard, or an Image. When creating a post, if nothing is selected for Post Format, then the Post Format will automatically be assigned to the default selected here.

Press This: This is a little app that runs in your browser and lets you grab bits from the Web. You can use this to add your own content for posts on your website. (See page 104.)

Post via e-mail: This is a little feature that will allow you to publish emails as blog posts. However, to achieve this you will need help from your email host to provide you with settings. If you are not using this setting, then leave the defaults in place.

Reading Settings

The Reading Settings are there to display how you want things to appear to the user of your website.

To access these, select **Settings** > **Reading.**

Reading Settings

Front page displays	◉ Your latest posts
	○ A static page (select below)
	Front page: — Select —
	Posts page: — Select —
Blog pages show at most	10 posts
Syndication feeds show the most recent	10 items

Front page displays: This is rather an important setting with regard to your website design. From here you select whether you want your front page to display your latest posts, or another static page that you have created. If you select a static page, then you must select which page you want to use for the homepage. You must also select the page you want to use as your posts page.

Blog pages show at most: This is the maximum number of posts you want to display per page. The default is 10. However, you can change this to whatever you like.

Syndication feeds show the most recent: This is the number of posts that the user will see if they download one of your feeds. The default is 10.

For each article in a feed, show: This will determine whether or not you show the full text from your post or just a summary on your blog/post page.

Search Engine Visibility: You might want to use this while your website or blog is still in development. It will stop search engines from indexing the site.

Hot tip

Unless you are building a blog, try to set your homepage as a static page.

To add an RSS Feed to your website: Go to **Appearance** > **Widgets**.

Drag the RSS Feed Widget from the left hand side (Available Widgets) to one of your Widget areas on the right.

Fill out the details in the **RSS Feed Widget Box**:

Enter the RSS feed URL here: *This will be http://www.yourdomain.com/feed/*

Give the feed a title.

How many items would you like to display?

Display item content? *Tick this box if you want the story to display some of the content underneath.*

Display item author if available?

Display item date?

Click **Save**.

Discussion Settings

The Discussion Settings are there for you to control how other users interact with your website or blog.

These can be accessed by selecting **Settings > Discussion.**

Default Article Settings: There are three tick boxes here:

Default article settings

- [ ] Attempt to notify any blogs linked to from the article
- [ ] Allow link notifications from other blogs (pingbacks and trackbacks)
- [ ] Allow people to post comments on new articles

(These settings may be overridden for individual articles.)

Attempt to notify any blogs linked to from the article: If you choose to tick this box, then your blog will send out pings and trackbacks to other articles.
Allow link notifications from other blogs (pingbacks and trackbacks): If you tick this box, then your blog will accept trackbacks from other blogs.
Allow people to post comments on new articles: This tick box is self explanatory, if you have the box ticked then it will allow users to post comments on new articles on your website.

Other Comment settings: This small section will control your comment settings for your website.

Other comment settings

- [ ] Comment author must fill out name and e-mail
- [x] Users must be registered and logged in to comment
- [ ] Automatically close comments on articles older than 14 days
- [x] Enable threaded (nested) comments 5 levels deep
- [ ] Break comments into pages with 50 top level comments per page and the last

Comments should be displayed with the older comments at the top of each page

Comment author must fill out name and e-mail: This first tick box will determine whether or not the user has to fill out name and email when posting a comment.
Users must be registered and logged in to comment: This box determines whether or not the user has to be registered or logged in to comment – this all depends on how you feel is best to monitor your comments.
Automatically close comments on articles older than: This tick box, if selected, will automatically close comments on articles or posts older than a certain amount of days. You can choose the amount of days yourself.

Trackbacks and pingbacks are methods for alerting websites that you have linked to them.

...cont'd

Enable threaded (nested) comments: This tick box will allow nested comments – this usually comes into play when users respond to other comments. You will need to choose how many levels deep you wish to use for this. This can affect your theme layout so try to restrict it to as low as you can.

Break comments into pages with: If your website is getting a lot of comments, then this option lets you break your comments section up by placing a set amount over a number of pages. Choose how many top level comments you want per page and whether or not you want the first or last comment page displayed by default.

Email me whenever: You will receive an email whenever anybody posts a comment or when a comment is held for moderation if you choose to select both tick boxes.

E-mail me whenever
Anyone posts a comment
A comment is held for moderation

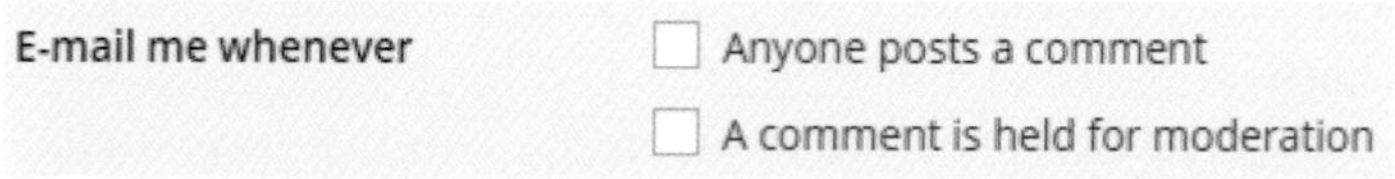

Before a comment appears: You can choose here whether or not a comment has to be manually approved by yourself before it is published, and also whether or not a comment author must already have had a previously approved comment to have a further comment shown automatically.

Comment Moderation: You can choose here to hold comments if they contain a certain amount of links. In the box you can type keywords in the box, and if the user who comments has one of those keywords in the comment, then it will be held in moderation.

Comment Moderation
Hold a comment in the queue if it contains 2 or more links. (A common characteristic of comment spam is a large number of hyperlinks.)
When a comment contains any of these words in its content, name, URL, e-mail, or IP, it will be held in the moderation queue. One word or IP per line. It will match inside words, so "press" will match "WordPress".

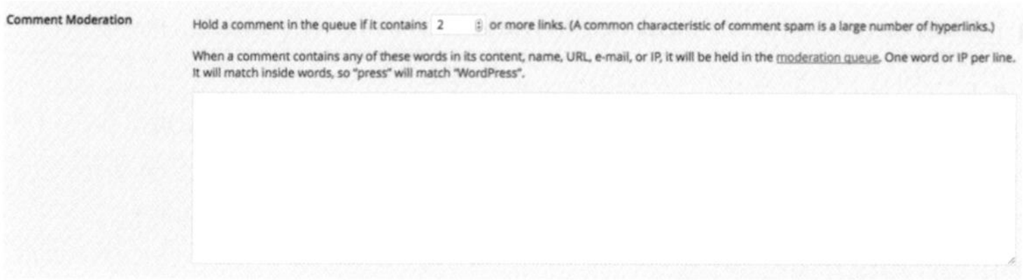

For example if you put "biscuit' in the word box, and a user posted a comment saying "I like biscuits", then the comment would be held in the moderation queue and would need to be approved.

Comment Blacklist: This box works in a similar fashion to the Comment Moderation box. However, in this case you can put keywords into the Comment Blacklist box and if a user comments with one of those words, then it will be marked as spam.

Comment Blacklist

When a comment contains any of these words in its content, name, URL, e-mail, or IP, it will be marked as spam. One word or IP per line. It will match inside words, so "press" will match "WordPress".

For example, if you put "jam" in the comment blacklist, and a user made a comment on a post saying "I like jam" then it would be marked as spam.

Avatars

An avatar is something that appears by your name on a blog or website. You might have noticed them on forums.

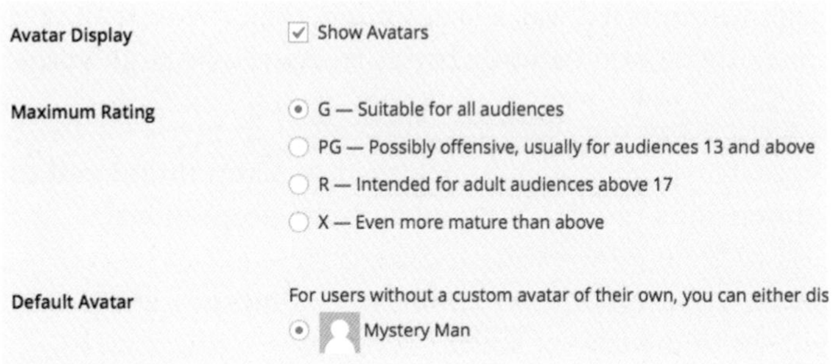

Avatar Display — Show Avatars

Maximum Rating
- G — Suitable for all audiences
- PG — Possibly offensive, usually for audiences 13 and above
- R — Intended for adult audiences above 17
- X — Even more mature than above

Default Avatar — For users without a custom avatar of their own, you can either dis
- Mystery Man

Avatar Display: You can choose to show avatars on your website or blog.

Maximum Rating: We all know about movie ratings right? Well this works in the same way with avatars. Choose the maximum rating level of avatars for your website. This is all going to depend on your audience.

Default Avatar: This is for users who have not chosen their own custom avatar. You are able to select a generic logo for them until they decide to use their own.

Media Settings

These settings will control how media is displayed on your WordPress website. You can access Media Settings by going to **Settings > Media.**

Image sizes

The sizes listed below determine the maximum dimensions in pixels to use when adding an image to the Media Library.

Thumbnail size	Width 150 Height 150 ☑ Crop thumbnail to exact dimensions (normally thumbnails are proportional)
Medium size	Max Width 300 Max Height 300
Large size	Max Width 1024 Max Height 1024

Image Sizes:
We went through adding Media and Images back in Chapter Four. The Media Library refers to three images sizes (Thumbnail, Medium and Large). Don't forget that WordPress will keep the settings from the last time you used them. So, for example, if the last image you inserted was a large image, then the next time you insert one, it will automatically be set to insert as a large image.

In this section you can select the dimensions in pixels for those three sizes. It is a good idea to tick the box **Crop thumbnail to exact dimensions** (normally thumbnails are proportional).

Most of us will usually insert an image as a full size image, as you can then set to the correct scale.

Uploading Files: If you tick the box, it will organize your uploads into month- and year-based folders.

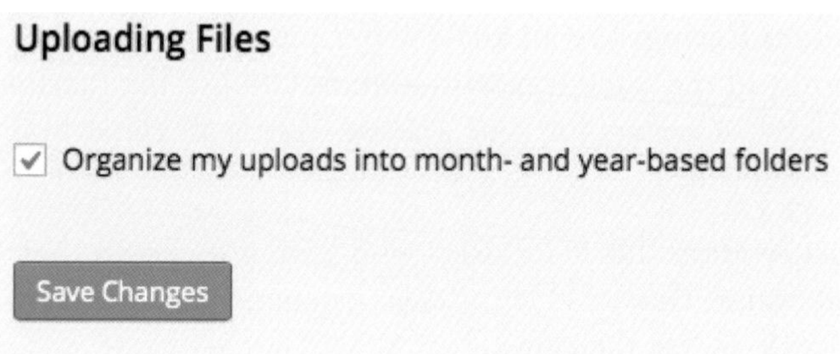

Permalinks Settings

This section allows you to set up the structure for your WordPress URLs. You can access these settings by clicking **Settings > Permalinks.**

Common Settings: You have six options here for the structure of your URLs. Most people will choose **Post name**, as this keeps the URL much simpler. You can see the examples set out in the screenshot and choose from there which one you want to you use.

Try to use Post name for your permalinks settings, as it will do better for your search engine optimization.

Optional: This gives you the opportunity to create custom structures for category and tag URLs. The default structure will be used if you leave these blank. The default structure for the category will look something like the URL below.

http://yoursite.com/category/WordPress

Category base	
Tag base	
Product category base	product-category
Product tag base	product-tag
Product attribute base	

Tools

We are now going to have a look at the Tools section in WordPress starting with Available Tools. There won't be too many tools in here initially, although when you install plugins some more tools may appear. Let's get started by going to **Tools > Available Tools.**

Available Tools

Press This will probably be the only tool you have here to start with. Press This is a little app that you can add to your Bookmarks Tab. Once you have it installed, while you are browsing you can select some text and then just click the **Press This** bookmark. This then brings up a pop up window where you can edit the content and save or publish as a post.

Import

The Import section can be used to import posts or comments from another blogging system. You can also install content from a WordPress export file.

For example, if you have posts that you want to import from Tumblr, then you can click **Tumblr** and it will bring up a Tumblr Importer.

Blogger

Blogroll

Categories and Tags Converter

LiveJournal

Movable Type and TypePad

RSS

Tumblr

WooCommerce Tax Rates (CSV)

WordPress

Export

Export can be used to export your WordPress content to an XML file. You can choose to export everything or just certain sections like Posts or Pages. This can then be imported into another WordPress installation.

For example, if you want to export your posts, then select **Posts** and click **Download Export File**.

8 SEO & Social Media

This chapter explains how to make your WordPress website more SEO friendly, and explains how you can add social media elements.

WordPress SEO by Yoast

One of the top reasons for developing websites with WordPress is the SEO aspect. There are dozens of amazing SEO plugins out there to help you optimize your website. This helps Google rank these websites higher compared with the sites developed in contemporary CMSs.

Search Engine Optimization (SEO) is a technique to help your website rank higher on search engines, such as Google, for particular keywords.

One such plugin is the WordPress SEO by Yoast. The Yoast plugin can be used to improve the on-page SEO of any WordPress website.

Installing WordPress SEO by Yoast Plugin

Download directly from the plugin's developer's site at **https://yoast.com/WordPress/plugins/seo/**

Or go to the WordPress Dashboard, go to the Plugins menu and install it from there

Install Now

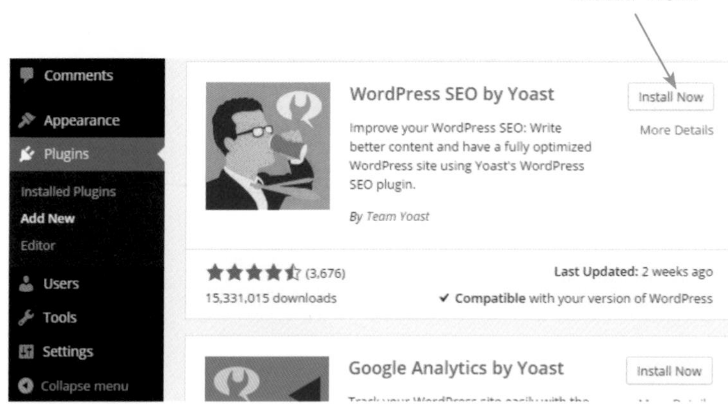

Once the plugin is installed, if you add a new post or page to your website, you will notice that a window appears below the post or page.

General
The general tab contains basic SEO options for your website:

The **Snippet Preview** shows how your website will appear on a search engine's page.

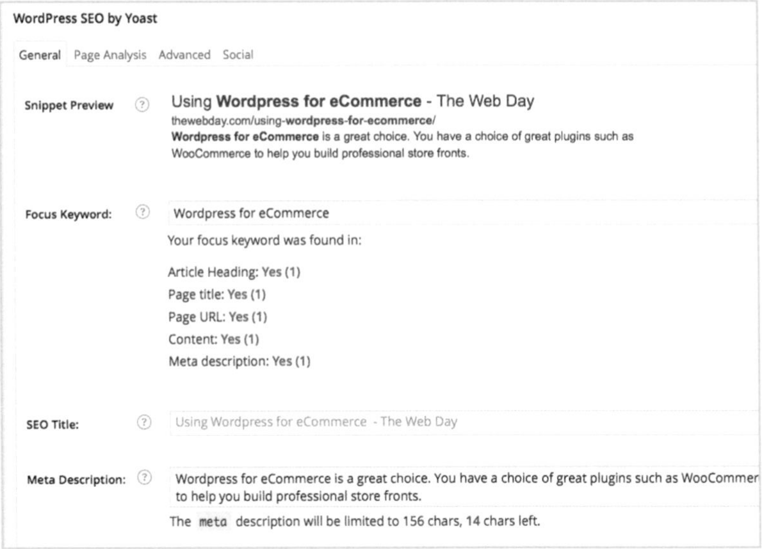

WordPress SEO by Yoast

General Page Analysis Advanced Social

Snippet Preview: Using **Wordpress for eCommerce** - The Web Day
thewebday.com/using-**wordpress-for-ecommerce**/
Wordpress for eCommerce is a great choice. You have a choice of great plugins such as WooCommerce to help you build professional store fronts.

Focus Keyword: Wordpress for eCommerce
Your focus keyword was found in:
Article Heading: Yes (1)
Page title: Yes (1)
Page URL: Yes (1)
Content: Yes (1)
Meta description: Yes (1)

SEO Title: Using Wordpress for eCommerce - The Web Day

Meta Description: Wordpress for eCommerce is a great choice. You have a choice of great plugins such as WooCommer to help you build professional store fronts.
The `meta` description will be limited to 156 chars, 14 chars left.

In **Focus Keyword**, the keyword against which you want to optimize your post is entered. For instance, in the above screenshot, the keyword "Wordpress for eCommerce" has been entered. You can see that a summary of the keyword appears under the text box which shows keyword stats. It contains information such as the number of times the keyword has been used in the Article Heading, Page Title, URL, Content and Meta Description.

In **SEO Title** enter the title for your site. It should also include the keyword that you entered.

Finally, **Meta Description** is also extremely important and the keyword should be used in the meta description as well.

Page Analysis
Page Analysis is the next tab to the General tab in the Yoast plugin. This tab contains analysis and reports about the SEO of your post and it also recommends how the SEO can be improved. For instance, for the keywords and content you entered in the General tab, Page Analysis displays the following information:

It can be seen from the screenshot that the page analysis report contains some comments and recommendations that are categorized by different colored circles. Red means that you need to pay particular attention to this item.

...cont'd

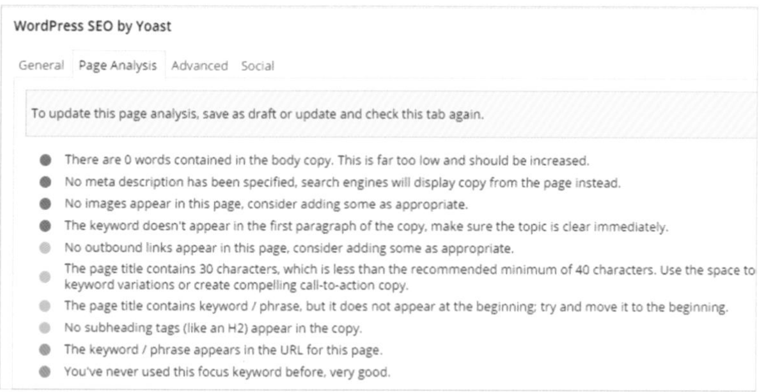
WordPress SEO by Yoast
General
Page Analysis
Advanced
Social
To update this page analysis, save as draft or update and check this tab again.
There are 0 words contained in the body copy. This is far too low and should be increased.
No meta description has been specified, search engines will display copy from the page instead.
No images appear in this page, consider adding some as appropriate.
The keyword doesn't appear in the first paragraph of the copy, make sure the topic is clear immediately.
No outbound links appear in this page, consider adding some as appropriate.
The page title contains 30 characters, which is less than the recommended minimum of 40 characters. Use the space to
keyword variations or create compelling call-to-action copy.
The page title contains keyword / phrase, but it does not appear at the beginning; try and move it to the beginning.
No subheading tags (like an H2) appear in the copy.
The keyword / phrase appears in the URL for this page.
You've never used this focus keyword before, very good.

Orange depicts that you should address this problem for better SEO. For instance, if your Page Analysis says that keyword density of the post is 0.39%, then you should improve that. Yellow means this is okay but there is room for improvement and finally, green is a symbol of appreciation for your SEO efforts.

To see the overall SEO rating for your post, go to the Publish window located at the top right of the post window.

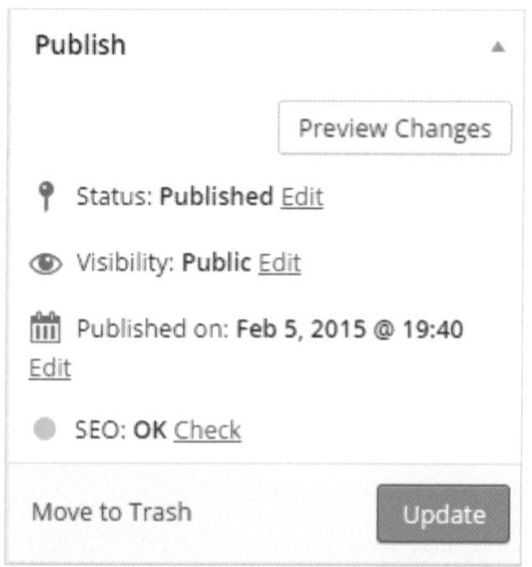
Publish
Preview Changes
Status: Published Edit
Visibility: Public Edit
Published on: Feb 5, 2015 @ 19:40
Edit
SEO: OK Check
Move to Trash
Update

Hot tip

Try to aim for an SEO green light in the Publish window.

In this example, the overall SEO for the post is OK. To improve the SEO of the post, you need to follow the instructions under the Page Analysis tab, save or update the post and again check the overall SEO of the post. Repeat the process, until you get a green circle here.

Advanced

The advanced tab contains some of the most advanced and powerful SEO options. These settings are usually done at website level. However, the Yoast plugin allows you to perform these functionalities at post or page level.

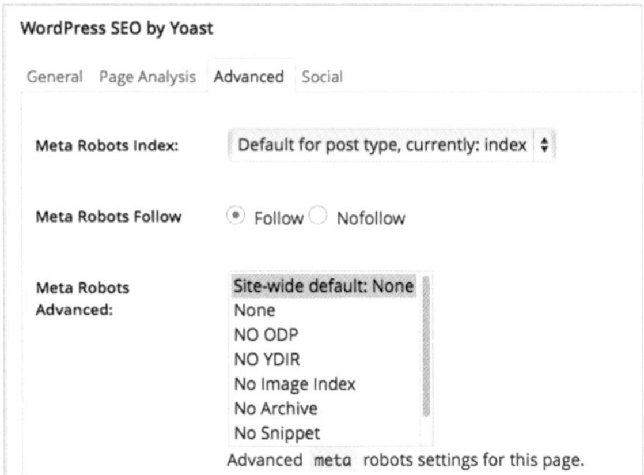

There are many advanced options for your post or page. Here are the most important ones:

Meta Robots Index: If you want search engines to index your page then you would select **index**. If you select **noindex** then this will disallow search engines from showing this page in their results.

Meta Robots Follow: If you choose **Follow**, then it tells the search engine robots to follow the links on the page, whether they can index it or not. By choosing **NoFollow** it will tell the search engine robots to not follow any links on the page at all.

Include in Sitemap: You can choose whether or not you want the page to be included in the sitemap (see page 157), this is regardless of any Meta Robot settings.

Canonical URL: You might have two pages with very similar content on the same URL, so you need to decide which is the preferred version so that the search engines can understand which is the preferred one when it comes to rankings. You can leave this blank if you don't have another page that is similar.

301 Redirect: A 301 redirect simply means the original old URL has been permanently moved. So you can specify a new URL here to redirect to.

...cont'd

Social

The last tab of the Yoast SEO WordPress plugin is the Social tab. Unlike previously mentioned tabs, this tab doesn't contain options for on-page SEO. Here, all the social media related options are specified. This is shown below:

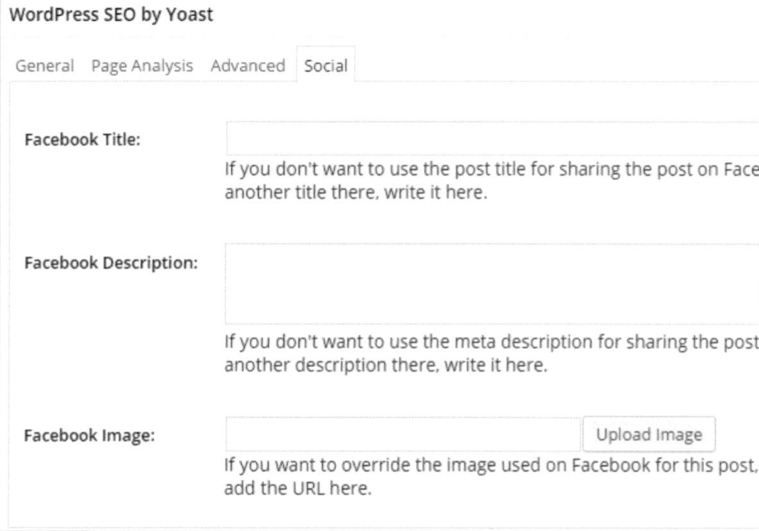

When people share your content on Facebook, you want to make sure the content is attractive, try and make the description as appealing as possible.

These options specify the behavior of the page or post when they are shared on social media platforms. For instance, you can set the Facebook Title and Description for the posts. This title will appear on Facebook when the post is shared there, along with the description. You can also upload the image to be displayed alongside the Facebook post.

If you entered "I love sandwiches" as the post title name, but in the social section you put "Sandwiches rule!" in the Facebook Title box, then on Facebook it would appear as "Sandwiches rule!" rather than the post title. The same applies with the description.

Social Media Overview

Social Media is everywhere these days. Whether you are browsing an online magazine or watching a video on YouTube, you will be sure to see a share button of some kind. Most people will now have some kind of social media account whether it be Facebook, Twitter, LinkedIn, or one of the other sites. This is why it is even more important for you and your users to be able to share content.

Here are some interesting statistics (source: *jeffbullas.com*) that show just how important Social Media is:

- **72% of all Internet users are now active on Social Media**
- **There are now over 1.15 billion Facebook users, over 550 million Twitter users, over 1 billion with Google+ enabled accounts**
- **70% of marketers used Facebook to gain new customers and 34% of marketers use Twitter to successfully generate leads**
- **23% of Facebook users log in at least five times per day**

These statistics are changing all the time, even while you read this book.

Improving Social Media Presence

When building a website, it is important to think of ways that users can discover and share your content. Users find a lot of good articles in their Facebook and Twitter feeds. Here are some ways your social media presence can be improved:

- Add sharing buttons to your content, so that users only need to click a button to share the content via their Social Media account.
- Create Social Media accounts for your own organization.
- Add Follow, Like Us buttons etc. on your page, so that users can start following your feeds.
- Interact with your users by answering their questions or queries.
- Create great content for users to read, as they will keep coming back for more.

Check out Online Marketing for Small Businesses in easy steps for more on social media marketing.

Share Buttons

Share buttons are a good way for users to be able to share content from your WordPress website. We suggest a great plugin called **WP Share Buttons & Analytics by GetSocial**, which will make it easy for you to add these share buttons to your posts.

To install this:

1. Go to **Plugins > Add New**
2. Search for **WP Share Buttons & Analytics by GetSocial**
3. Install and activate the plugin

WP Share Buttons & Analytics by *GetSocial*
Install Now
More Details
Add social media sharing buttons from the most popular networks to track user activity, increase traffic, improve SEO, and follow conversions.
By Getsocial, S.A.
(1)
1,002 downloads
Last Updated: 1 week ago
Compatible with your version of WordPress

4. Now it's installed, go to **GetSocial** on your Dashboard to set up your buttons

5. Enter your URL and email address to get your API Key

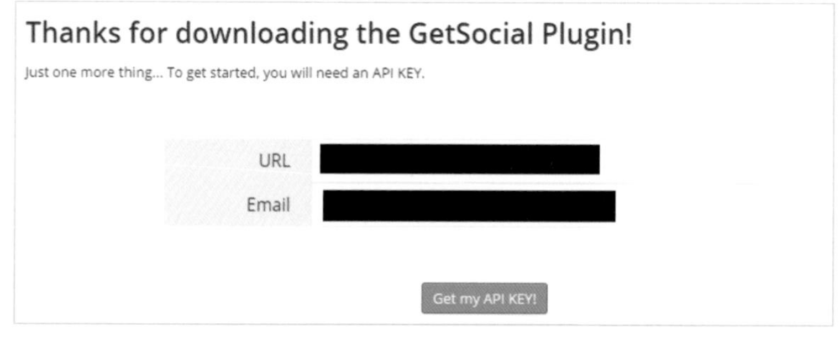

Thanks for downloading the GetSocial Plugin!
Just one more thing... To get started, you will need an API KEY.
URL
Email
Get my API KEY!

An API key is a long code used to identify you as a user for a particular plugin. It is likely that there will be a huge numbers of users using a particular plugin, so the API key gives the WordPress plugin developer a way to know the identity of each user so they can maintain a log.

6. Scroll down to the **Horizontal Sharing bar** box and click **+Add**

7. Fill out the form to set up your buttons

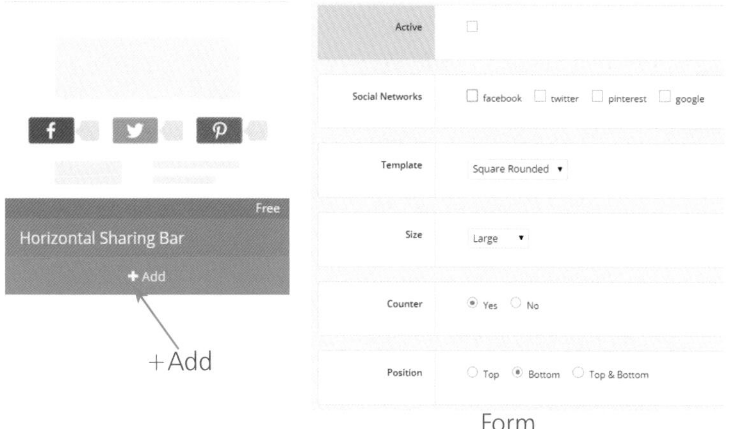

Form

Hot tip

It is best to keep your social buttons at the bottom of your content. This way you will be keeping the page tidy and the user can share straight after they have read the content.

Active: You will need to tick this box to activate the buttons.

Social Networks: Tick the boxes of the social networks you want your visitors to be able to share content on.

Template: Choose from one of the templates. You might want your social buttons to be square or round.

Size: Choose the size of the buttons.

Counter: If you choose to have a counter, it will display a number next to each social button. This number will let visitors know how many times the content has been shared.

Position: Choose the position of the buttons. It is usually best to keep them at the bottom.

As you fill out the form, you will be shown a preview of how the social buttons will look on your website.

8. Finally, click **Save Changes** to make your social buttons live

Twitter Feed

Hopefully you have set up a Facebook or Twitter page by now for your blog/website. If not – what are you waiting for? We demonstrated adding a Facebook like box, when we were talking about widgets. This is a great way to get users to like your page. We are now going to have a look at adding a Twitter Feed to your website, so that users can see your latest Tweets and get the chance to follow you.

1. Go to the Twitter website (**www.twitter.com**) and log in

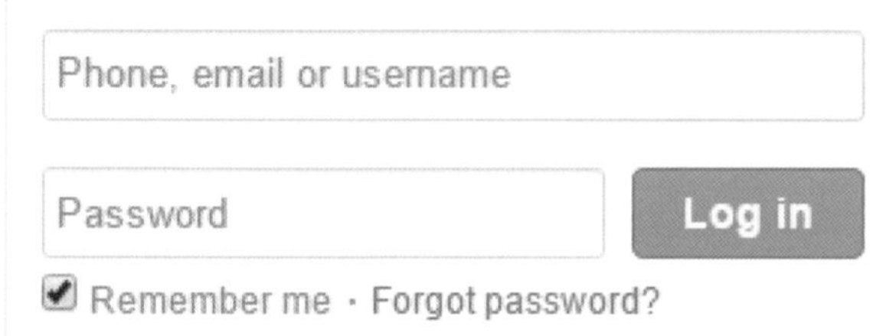

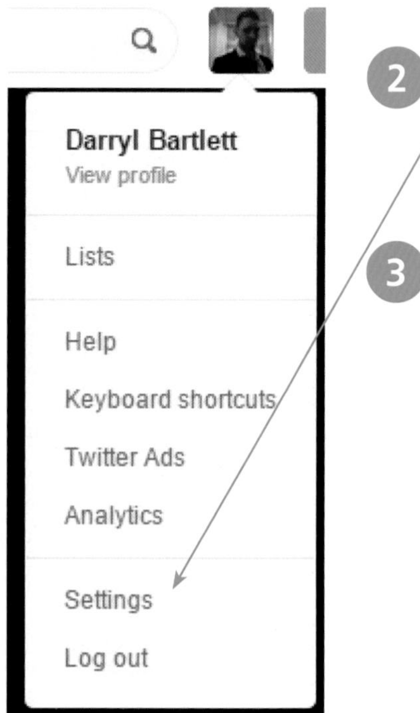

2. Click your profile picture on the top right and select **Settings** from the dropdown menu

3. You are now faced with a number of options down the left hand side of the page. Click the **Widgets** option, which will take you through to a page of widgets. This is likely to be empty unless you are already using some. This is where you will set up new widgets for your website

Widgets 

Widgets
Create and manage your widgets.
Create new

4. Select **Create new** on the top right hand side

5. Now you need to configure the Twitter widget that you want to create

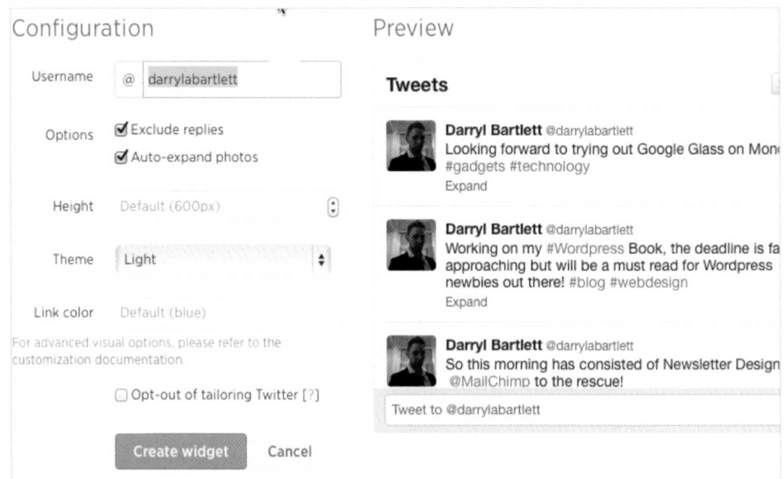

Username: This is the name of the Twitter account you want to use.

Options: Here you can select a couple of tick boxes; the first one will exclude the replies in your widget, and the second one allows you to auto expand any photos that are shared.

Height: You can leave this at the default 600px or enter your own height for the widget.

Theme: You have two choices here; you can use the light or dark theme.

Link color: Finally, you can choose the link color for the links in your Tweets - the default is set to blue.

6. Finally, click **Create Widget** to generate the code. Make sure you copy the code you are given

...cont'd

7. Go back to WordPress and head to your Dashboard. Usually the best place to put Twitter feeds is in a widget area (right hand side, left hand side, footer etc.)

8. Go to **Appearance > Widgets**

9. Drag over a text widget from the left hand side to one of your widget areas. A text widget looks like this:

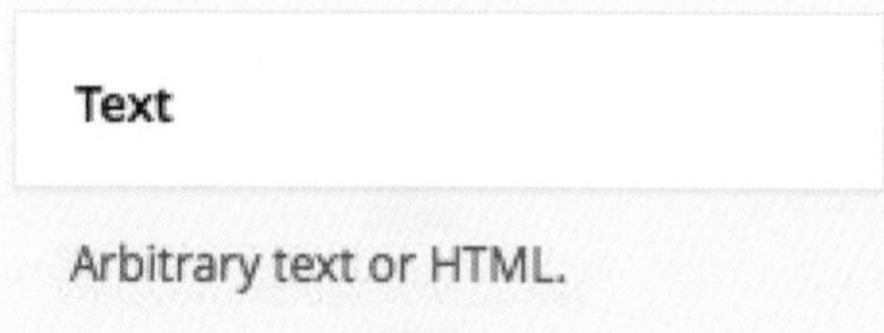

10. Now, in that widget, add a title, and paste your code into the big text area

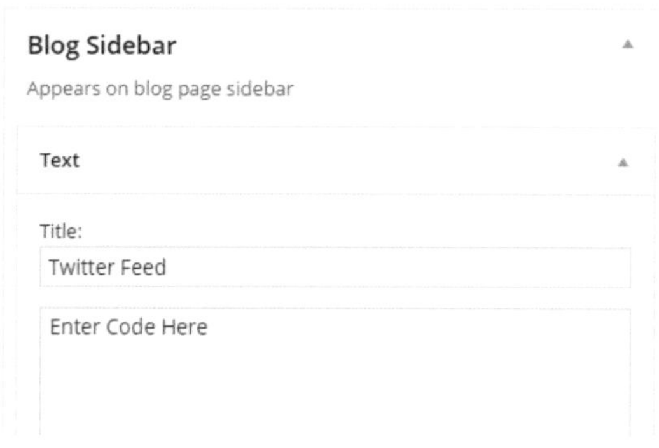

You can go back and alter your widget at anytime.

11. Finally, click **Save** and you should now find your widget on your live website!

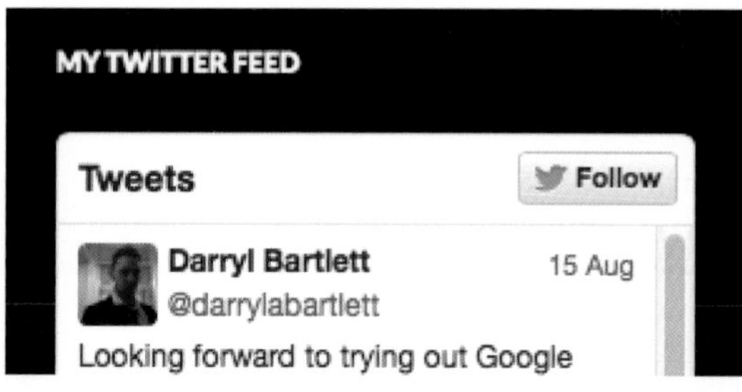

Instagram Photos

Sharing photos these days is a massive trend. Instagram allows you to share your daily adventures through the medium of images. If you are familar with Instagram, you may want to share your uploads on your WordPress website. Once again, there are some great plugins that can help you with this. One of these is called Instagram Feed. It allows you to add a shortcode to your Posts and Pages or even add them into widget areas. To install Instagram Feed:

1. Go to **Plugins > Add New**
2. Search for **Instagram Feed**
3. Install and Activate the plugin, just the same as you have done with previous plugins. You will now notice that Instagram Feed has appeared in your Dashboard, so click on it to get started

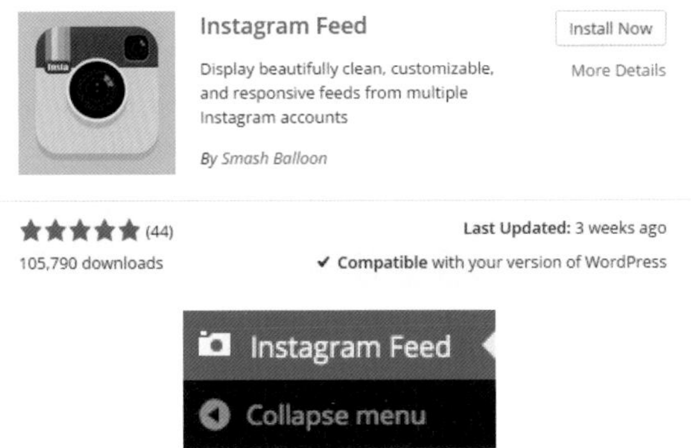

4. Log in with your Instagram ID – do this by clicking the **Log in and get my Access Token and User ID** button

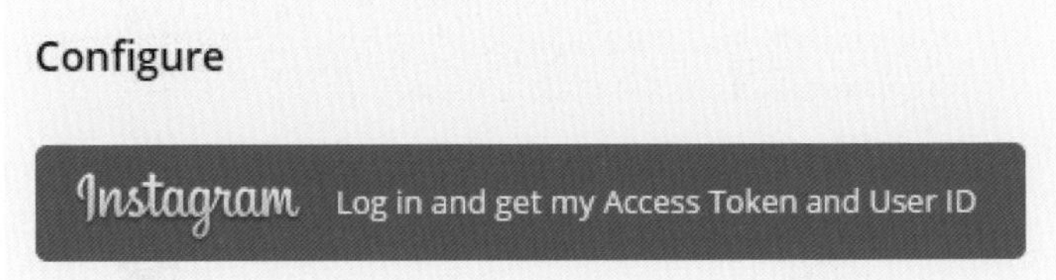

...cont'd

Remember that any future photos that you post to Instagram will automatically appear on your website or blog.

5. You will notice that the Access Token and User ID fields will automatically be filled in the top white box. You will need to copy these into the fields below that, as outlined below. The IDs have been blanked out in the example below. When you are happy, click the button at the bottom to **Save Changes**

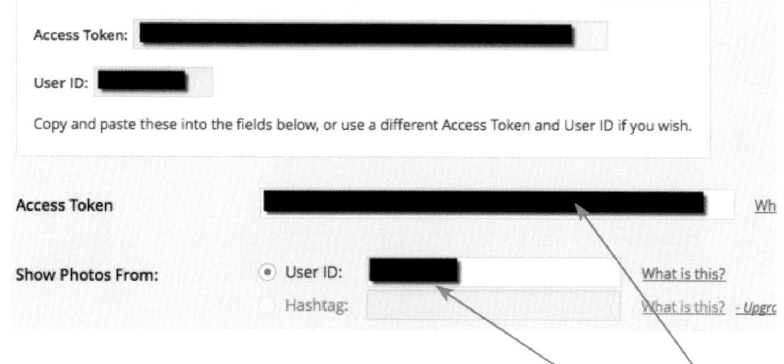

Paste Access Token and User ID into these fields

6. You can use the second tab (2. Customize) to personalize your Instagram widget. From here you are able to edit the width, height, background color, etc. You can also choose how you want to sort the photos and how many you want to show

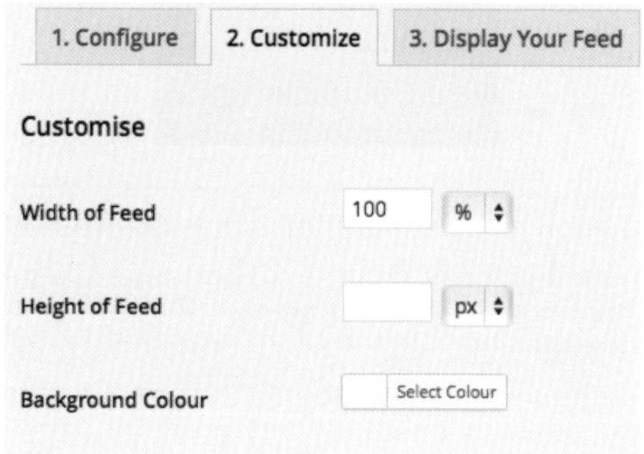

7. Finally, you will need to insert the following Instagram shortcode into your post, pages or widget

[instagram-feed]

9 User Interaction

This chapter explains various ways that users can interact with your website. It also covers setting up user membership and translation tools.

Comments

Allowing comments on your website or blog will encourage users to return to your site.

Comments are a good way for your users to reach out to you, and it allows you to build a two way communication with your visitors. It also allows you to build up a community, and encourage visitors to return to your website or blog. It is more common to see comments on a blog rather than a website. However, the importance of making sure there is a blog on any website seems to be rising.

One thing to bear in mind with regard to comments is that as well as managing them, you should allow both positive and negative comments. Users will respect you more for this.

Managing Comments

When users make comments through your website or blog, they will appear in the comments section of WordPress. To access this, click **Comments** from the Dashboard.

You will now be presented with a screen, which will show all your website comments. Remember that some comments will be spam (see page 122).

Along the top there are five different sections. All, Pending, Approved, Spam and Trash.

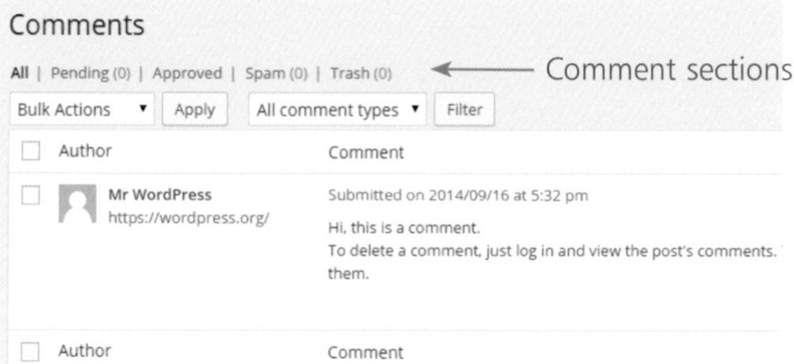

When your comments come in, they are likely to go into your pending section, and you will need to approve the comments before they go live.

You can change these various settings in **Discussion > Settings** (see page 100).

Approving Comments

To approve a comment, you will need to hover your mouse over the comment, and click the **Approve** link.

Approve | Reply | Quick Edit | Edit | Spam | Trash

Click to approve

Other Options

You will also see a number of other options:

Reply: This allows you to reply to the comment. The reply will become public on the website.

Quick Edit: This allows you to make a quick edit to the comment using a small window.

Edit: This will take you to a full sized page to edit the comment, this is useful if the comment is quite a long one.

Spam: This link will mark the comment as spam.

Trash: This will send the comment to the trash folder.

User Comment Editing

There is a plugin called Simple Comment Editing that allows anonymous users to edit their own comments within a certain period of time. This also applies to users who don't have the privileges to edit comments in the Dashboard. To install the Simple Comment Editing:

1. Go to **Plugins** > **Add New**
2. Type in Simple Comment Editing and click **Search Plugins**
3. Install and activate the plugin

Once the plugin is activated, users can edit their comments for up to five minutes after posting.

It is not advised to edit user comments without the permission of the author. The email address of the comment author is shown along with the comment, so you can get in contact with them easily.

Akismet & Spam

When it comes to spam, there is a good plugin called Akismet, which filters out the spam for you. Akismet will come pre-installed with WordPress, but you will need to set it up before it works.

1. Go to **akismet.com** and register for an API key
2. Go to **Settings > Akismet** from your Dashboard to enter your key

Manually enter an API key
If you already know your API key.
Use this key

In this day and age, you definitley need a plugin to sort through your spam. Akismet is a great choice and will save you a lot of time.

Once you have a Akismet account set up, your website will then be automatically be protected from spam, so if someone comments and the system recognizes it as spam, then it will automatically be placed in the spam folder.

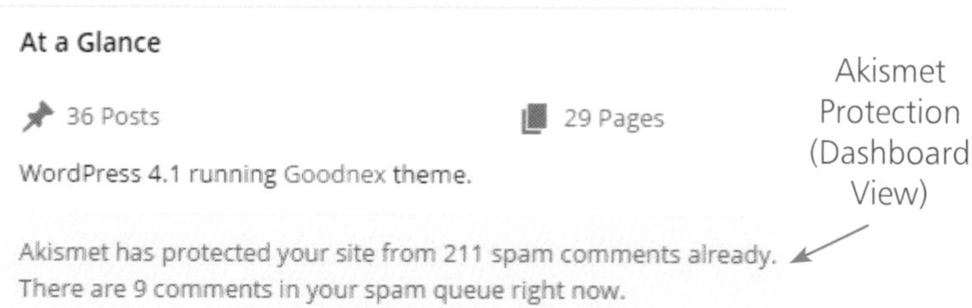

At a Glance
36 Posts
29 Pages
WordPress 4.1 running Goodnex theme.
Akismet has protected your site from 211 spam comments already.
There are 9 comments in your spam queue right now.

Akismet Protection (Dashboard View)

There is also a **Check for Spam** button in the comments section which you can press to check through all your current comments.

Check for Spam

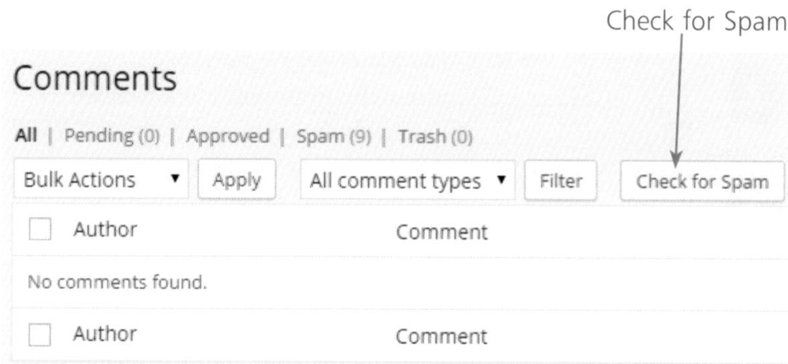

Forums

Thanks to WordPress plugins, it is possible to create online discussion forums with WordPress. Let's take a look at how you can integrate forums on to your WordPress website using a plugin called bbPress.

1. From the Dashboard go to **Plugins > Add New**

2. Search for a plugin called bbPress and install it

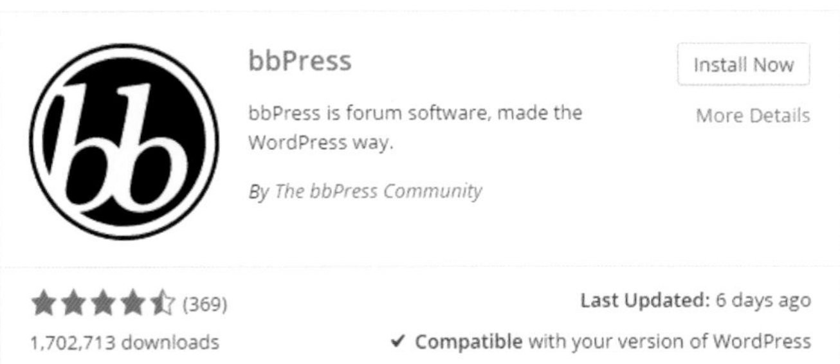

Try to create forums relevant to your website. Users will want to talk about issues relevant to your website content.

Setting up Forums

Now that you have the plugin installed, you are ready to start creating forums for your website. You will notice down the left hand side of the Dashboard there are three options that have been added (Forums, Topics, Replies).

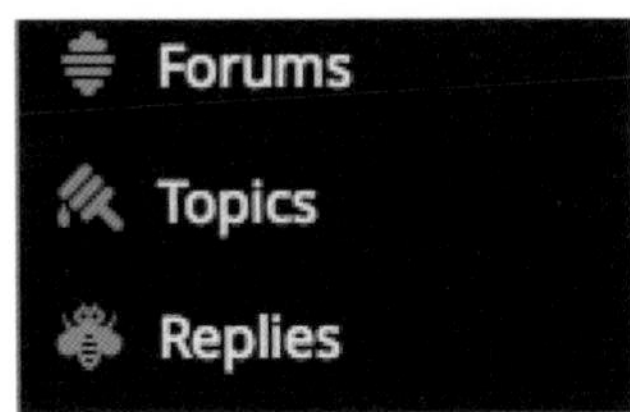

Forums: This is where you can add new forums and manage any exisiting ones.

Topics: This lists topics in every category. You can also add topics here or manage topic tags.

Replies: Here you can manage the replies to every post in each forum.

...cont'd

1. To create a new forum, click the **Forums** link

2. Click the **New Forum** button

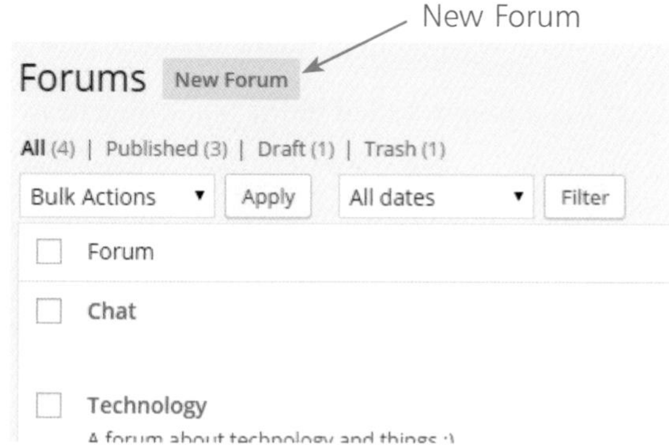

3. This process is as simple as setting up a regular post or page. Enter a title for the forum and a description

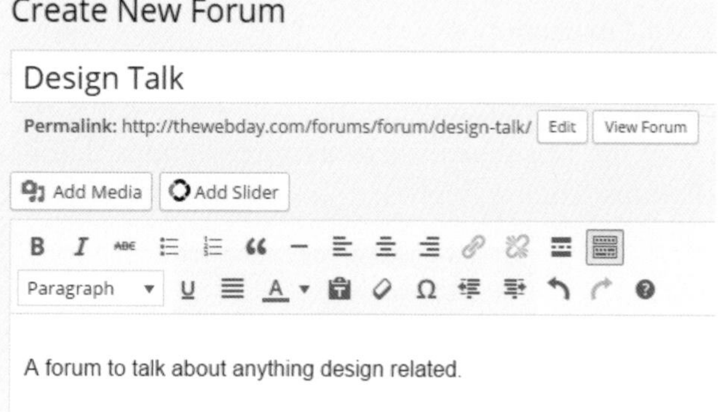

4. The last thing to do before you publish, is to set the forum attributes

Forum Attributes

Type: Forum

Status: Open

Visibility: Public

Parent: — No parent —

Order: 0

Type: Set as a Forum or Category.

Status: Here you can set the forum as Open or Closed. If the forum is open, then people can post new topics. If the forum is closed then no new topics can be posted although old topics will still be there to read.

Visibility: You can set whether you want the forum to be public, private or hidden.

Order: This is where you set the forum order. This determines the running order of the forums down the page.

Parent: If your forum is a sub forum, then set the parent here.

5 Click **Publish** to set up the forum

You will see when you go to the forums page *(http://www.yourdomain.com/forums/)*, that your forum is now displayed.

Forum

Design Talk

A forum to talk about anything design related.

Try to keep advertising forums to more active members, or you could end up with visitors spamming your forums.

If you first click on your forum, you will see that the forum is empty. This is because no topics have been set up yet by you or any of your users. You can create topics from the live site itself, or from the backend, which we will cover on page 127.

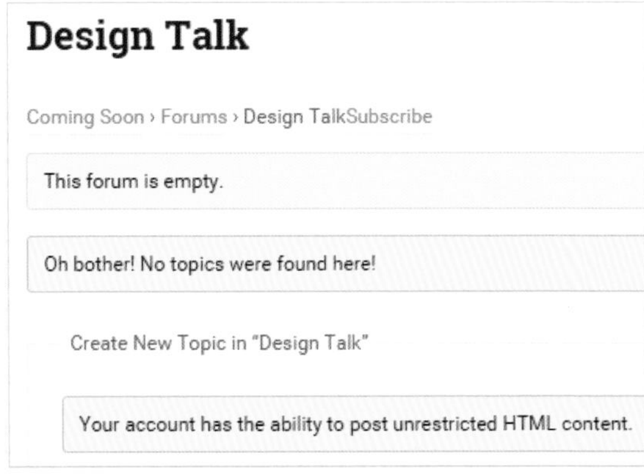

Design Talk
Coming Soon › Forums › Design TalkSubscribe
This forum is empty.
Oh bother! No topics were found here!
Create New Topic in "Design Talk"
Your account has the ability to post unrestricted HTML content.

...cont'd

Editing Existing Forums

It's very simple to edit existing forums, so if you need to change the title, description, status, visibility etc. then you can do it very easily.

1. Select **Forums > All Forums** from the Dashboard**.** This will display all the forums you have created

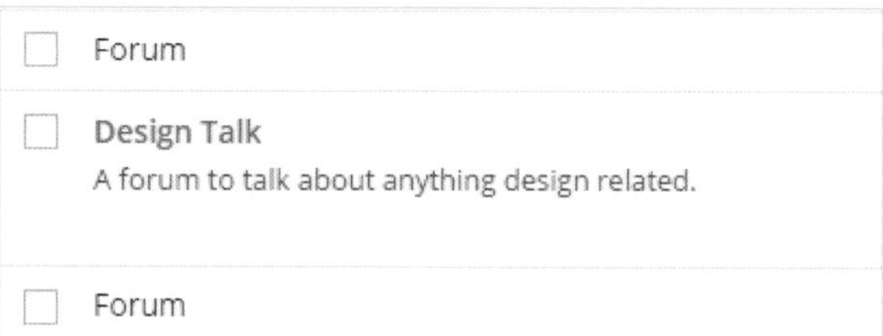

2. Click on the forum you wish to edit. This will bring up a page similar to when you created the forum. You can now make your changes. Don't forget to save your changes

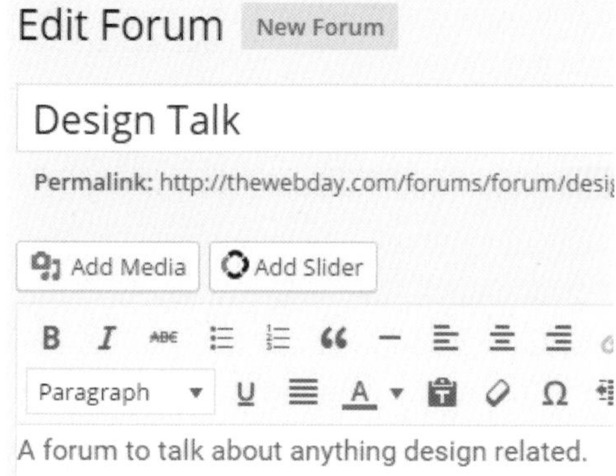

One thing to bear in mind when having a forum on your website, is that you will need to make sure users can register on your website.

Make sure you have ticked the Membership box under the **Settings > General** page.

Adding Topics

You may wish to let your users set up topics on your forum, but you can also create them yourself. You can do this from the front end as you will already be logged in. However let's go through the process of adding a topic from the back end.

Try to add a couple of topics to your forum before it goes live. This way it gives visitors something to talk about and will encourage them to post.

1. Click **Topics** from the Dashboard. This will display all the current topics in your forum

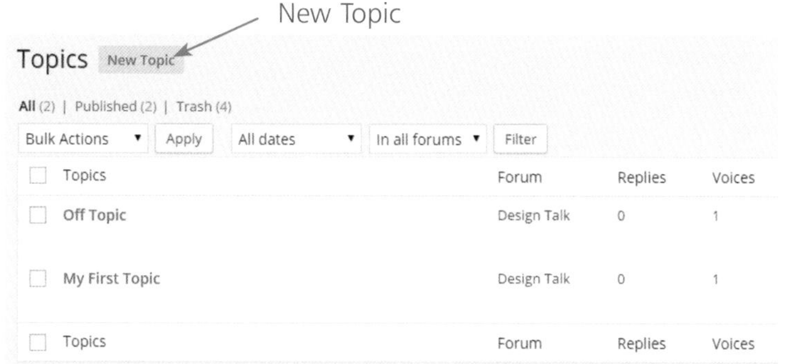

2. To add a new topic, click **New Topic**

Create New Topic
Random Topic
Permalink: http://thewebday.com/for
Add Media
Paragraph
Here is a topic!

3. Just like you did when you created a forum, you will need to create a topic name and a description

4. You will also need to set topic attributes

Topic Attributes
Type: Sticky
Status: Open
Forum: Design Talk

Type: This could be a regular topic, or you could use **Sticky** which appears at the top of that particular forum, or **Super sticky** which stays at the top of all forums.
Status: You will need to set this to Open.
Forum: Select which forum you want the topic to appear in.

...cont'd

5 Click **Publish** to make your topic live

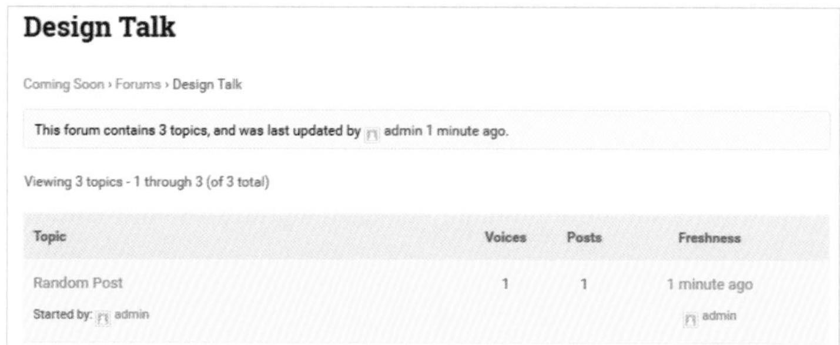

You will notice that the post has now appeared in the forum. In this case, a sticky post was created, which has appeared right at the top.

Editing Topics

When users add topics on your website you can easily monitor them by going to **Topics > All Topics** and going through each one. You are still able to change the status of each individual topic that a user adds.

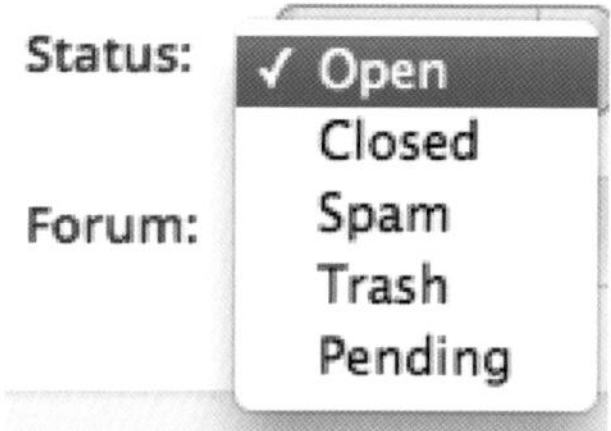

Replies

The Replies section is a good way to monitor replies to topics on your forums. All your replies will appear in the **Replies > All Replies** section, which appears in the Dashboard.

You can add replies yourself from here, although it is probably best to do this from the individual post on the live site, it also makes things less complex.

Contact Forms

Contact Forms have to be the most vital element when it comes to communicating with your website visitors. Every website should have one, whether it's a blog or a business website.WordPress has some great plugins to set contact forms up on your website. We are going to have a look at one called Contact Forms 7.
Let's get started.

Make sure your contact page and contact form can be easily spotted by visitors.

1. **Go to Plugins > Add New** from the Dashboard
2. Search for **Contact Form 7**, then Install and Activate the plugin
3. Once installed, you should have a new link on the left hand side of your dashboard called **Contact**. Go ahead and click this

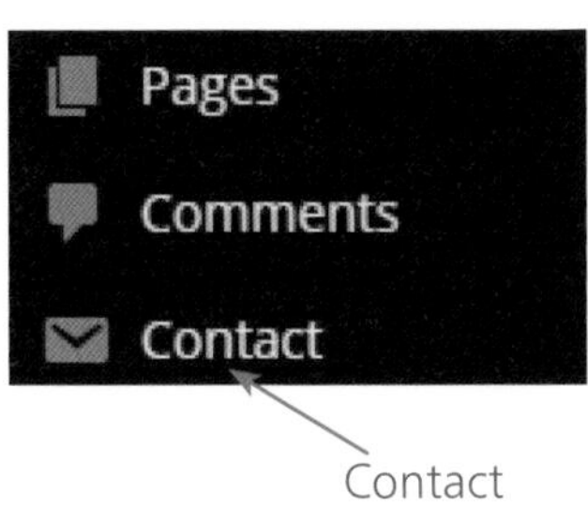

Contact

4. Click **Add New** from the top of the page

Contact Forms Add New

5. Choose a name for the contact form

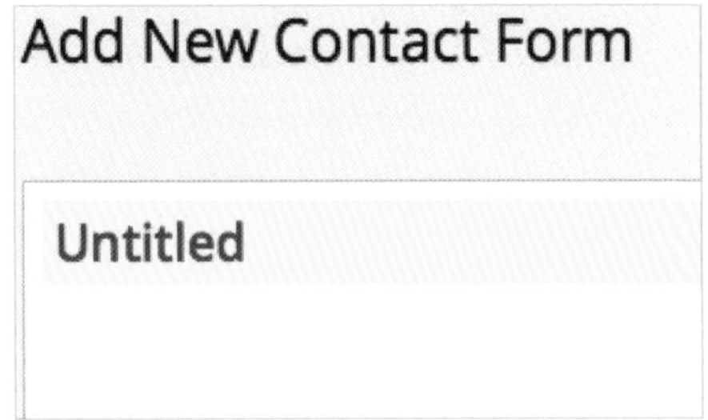

You will notice there is a form already made for you.

...cont'd

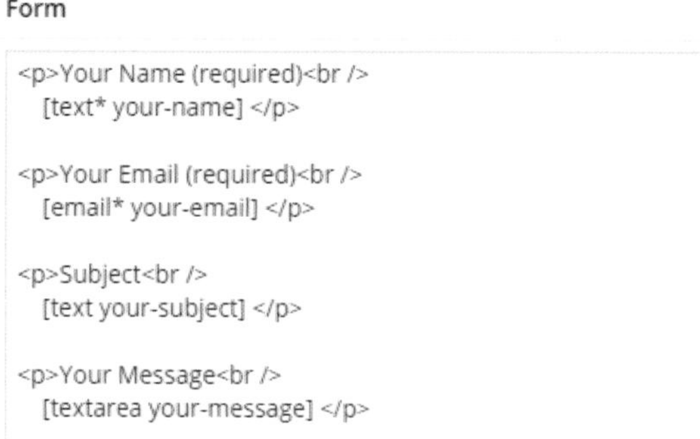

Form

```
<p>Your Name (required)<br />
  [text* your-name] </p>

<p>Your Email (required)<br />
  [email* your-email] </p>

<p>Subject<br />
  [text your-subject] </p>

<p>Your Message<br />
  [textarea your-message] </p>

<p>[submit "Send"]</p>
```

Try not to add too many fields to your form. Most people use name, email, phone and message.

6. Add your own field names between <p> </p>

7. **Mail:** The mail settings will be filled out already. Make sure the **To:** field is filled out with the address you want mail sent to

To:

bartlett_darryl@yahoo.co.uk

From:

[your-name] <[your-email]>

Subject:

[your-subject]

8. **Messages:** This section is used to set up some default messages, if the message contains errors, or if the messages fail to send, etc.

Sender's message was sent successfully

Your message was sent successfully. Thanks.

Sender's message was failed to send

Failed to send your message. Please try later or contact the administrator by another method.

Validation errors occurred

Validation errors occurred. Please confirm the fields and submit it again.

Some emails may come through to your spam folder. This is very much dependent on your email provider.

9. To finish you will need to click **Save.** You will be given a shortcode, which you can post into your pages/posts or even inside a widget. It will look something like the one below

Copy this code and paste it into your post, page or text widget content.

```
[contact-form-7 id="61" title="Hello"]
```

Website Translation

There may come a time where you want to expand your reach. Translating your website is a great way of reaching new readers or customers. There are various plugins that can help you make your website multilingual. One of the best ones is called gTranslate. It has three versions – Free, Pro and Enterprise. Upon installation of the plugin, your website will automatically be translated, making it simple and easy not just for you but also for your readers.

Installing gTranslate

1. Visit **www.gtranslate.net** and download the plugin

2. Go to **Plugins > Add New** from the WordPress Dashboard

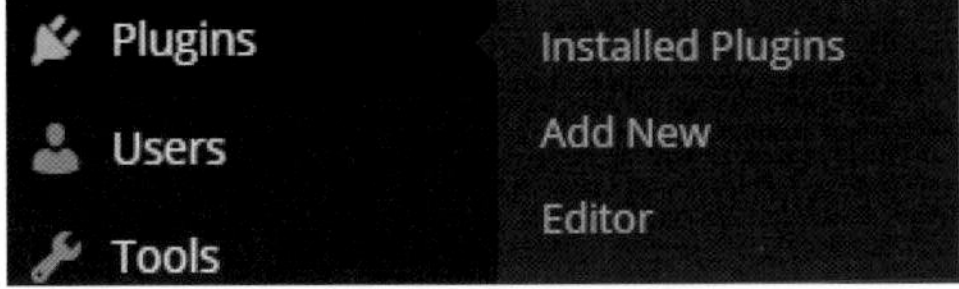

3. Select **Upload Plugin** at the top

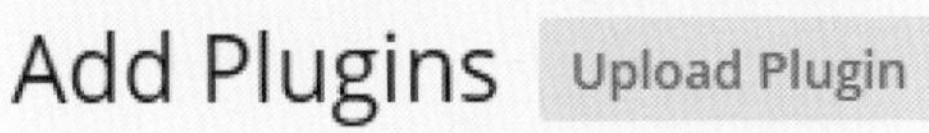

4. As you have done before, select **Choose File** and select the zip file that you downloaded from the gTranslate website

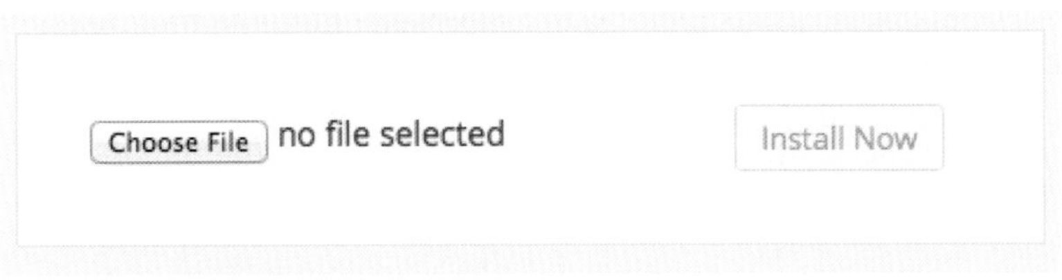

...cont'd

5. Click **Install Now.** Remember to activate the plugin so you can get it working straight away

Configuring gTranslate

1. Go to **Settings** > **GTranslate** from the WordPress Dashboard

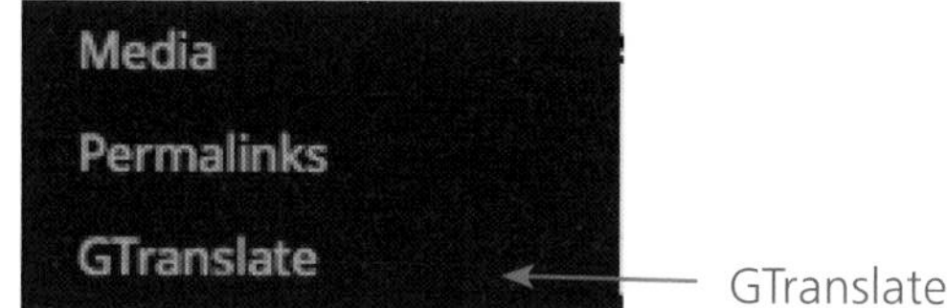

2. You will now be presented with a number of options with regard to how you want the translation to function

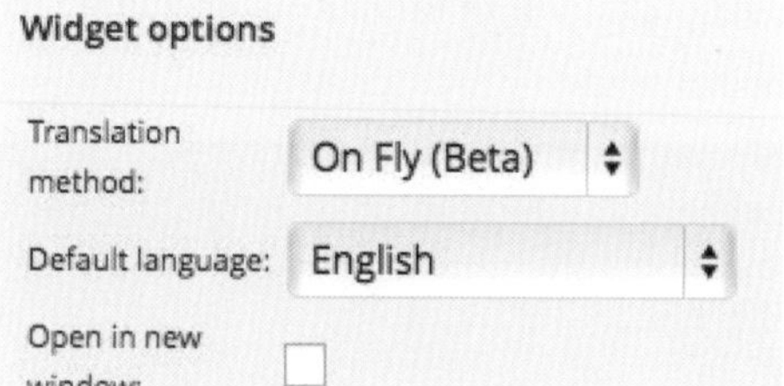

You will also see a preview of your gTranslate widget.

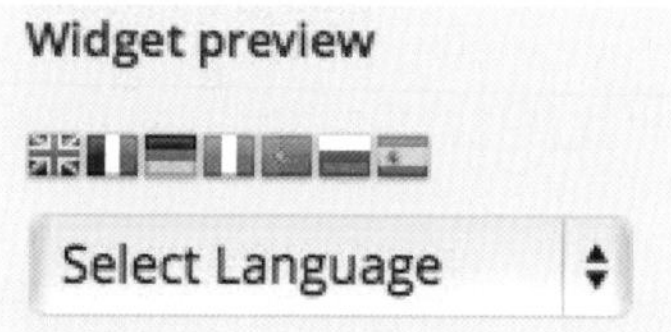

You can set things like flag size, whether or not you want the flags to show, flag languages, dropdown languages etc. You will also find your widget code here

3. When you are happy, click **Save Changes** at the bottom of the page

Inserting gTranslate using Widgets

There are a number of ways you can insert gTranslate on your website or blog. The best way is by inserting it as a widget. When you installed the gTranslate plugin, it automatically created a widget, ready for you to insert in a particular area on your webpage.

1. Head over to **Appearance** > **Widgets** from the WordPress Dashboard

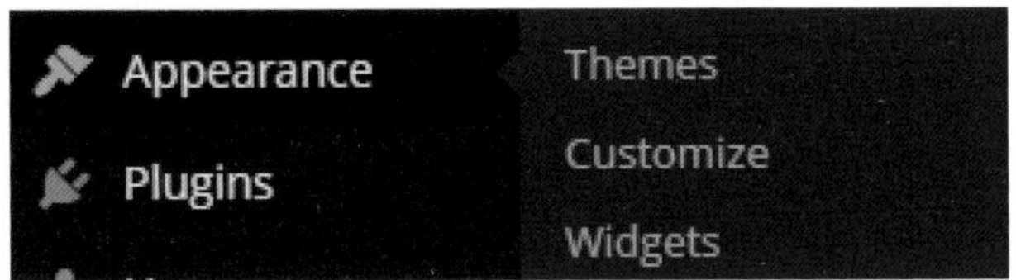

2. Drag the gTranslate widget over from the left-hand side to one of your sidebars on the right

GTranslate

Title:

Translate

Please go to Settings -> GTranslate for configuration.

Delete | Close   Save

3. Remember to set a title, and then click **Save**

Your widget should now appear on your live website, and the translation should work when you change language. You can make adjustments to the settings at any time.

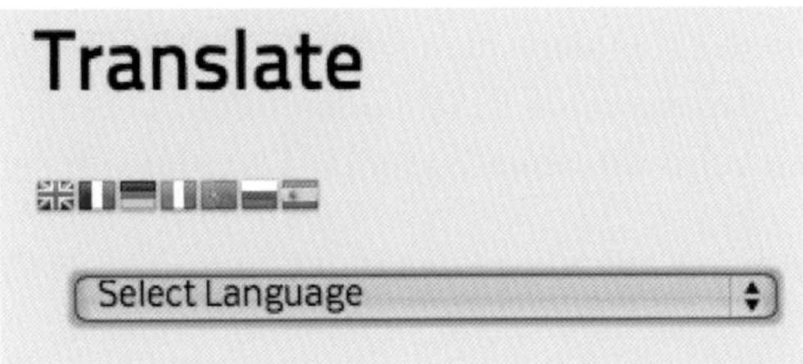

Try to position the widget in full view so that visitors can translate quickly and easily.

...cont'd

You can also add gTranslate to your PHP template files and to individual pages.

Inserting gTranslate inside pages or posts

1. Head over to one of your pages or posts by selecting **Pages** or **Posts** from your Dashboard and picking the page or post where you want to insert the gTranslate widget

Title

Our New Website

Title

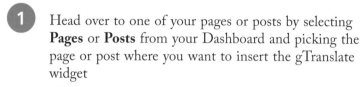

2. Now, insert the shortcode [gtranslate] into your post or page. Click **Update** when you are finished widget

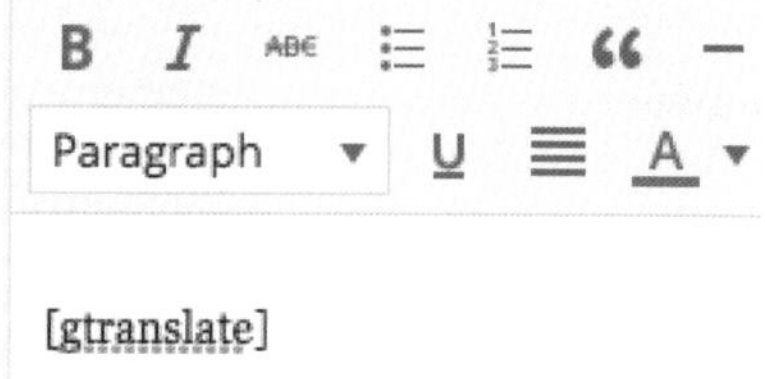

Inserting gTranslate into your PHP files

1. Go to **Appearance** > **Editor** from your WordPress Dashboard widget

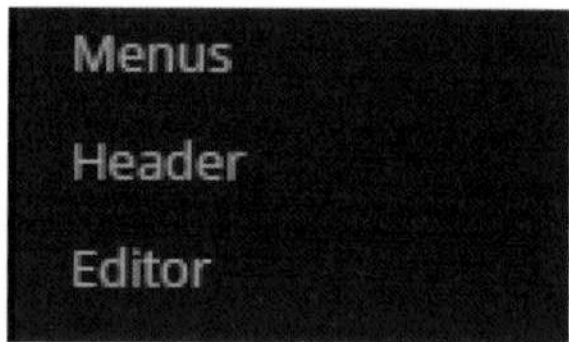

2. Select the template file (for example: header.php) and insert this piece of PHP code:
<?php echo do_shortcode('[GTranslate]'); ?>

```
<?php echo do_shortcode('[GTranslate]'); ?>
```

Not all themes will allow you access to the Editor area, so you may need to access the PHP file through FTP. You will be introduced to accessing your files through FTP on page 163.

Membership Levels

You may want to set up membership levels for your users. For example, you may have an educational website where users can download content or a premium area for paid users. There is a fantastic plugin for WordPress called Paid Memberships Pro which can help you with this.

Installing Paid Memberships Pro

1. From your Dashboard select **Plugins** > **Add New**
2. Search for **Paid Memberships Pro** and install like you have done with previous plugins

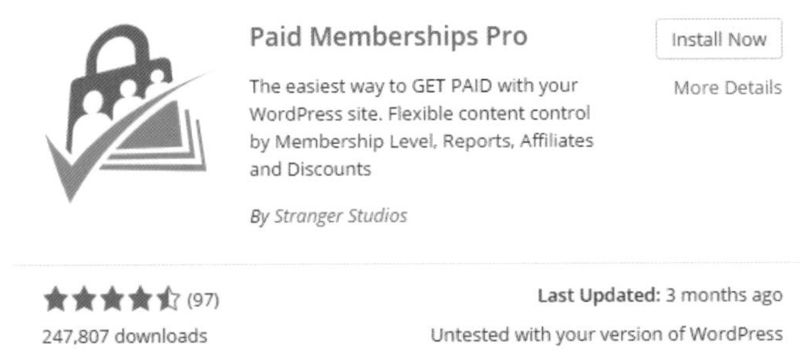

Paid Memberships Pro
Install Now
More Details
The easiest way to GET PAID with your WordPress site. Flexible content control by Membership Level, Reports, Affiliates and Discounts
By Stranger Studios
(97)
247,807 downloads
Last Updated: 3 months ago
Untested with your version of WordPress

3. Activate your plugin after installation
4. You should see on the Dashboard that there is now an option called **Memberships** as shown below

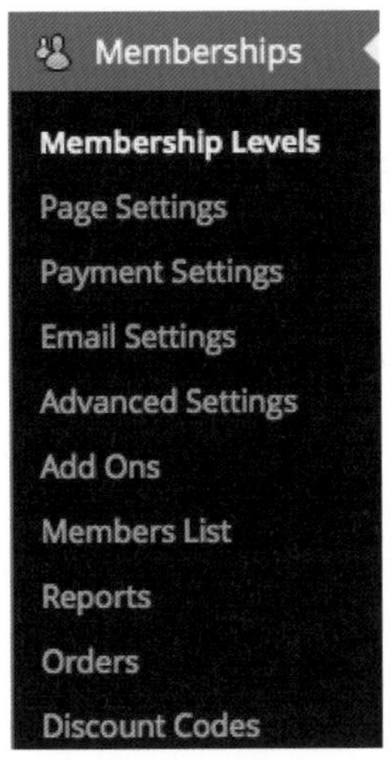

5. There are quite a few options here. Begin by selecting **Membership Levels** which is the first option and will allow you to begin setting up membership levels for your website

...cont'd

Add New Membership Level

1 Select **Add New Level**

Membership Levels Add New Level ← Add New Level

Add a membership level to get started.

ID Name Initial Payment

Set up your Membership Level using the following options:

Add New Membership Level

ID:

Name:

Description: Add Media

Paragraph

Name: Enter a name for your membership level.

Description: Enter a description – this needs to be something that the user will understand.

Confirmation Message: This is a message that will display to the user upon sign up.

Initial Payment: This amount is what the user will pay at signup. You are able to choose if this is a recurring payment.

Keep the descriptions simple and easy for the visitor to understand. They will want to know exactly what they are signing up for.

Disable New Signups: At first, you don't need to tick the box. You would only tick the box if you wanted to disable new signups to this particular membership.

Membership Expiration: Check this box to disable access when membership expires.

Content Settings/Categories: Here you can select what categories your membership covers. For example, you may have a Design membership that only design members can access.

2 Finish your settings by clicking **Save Level** which will complete the setup

Page Setup for Members Only

When you created your membership, you were able to set up post categories for particular memberships, but you also need to be able to set up pages to be visible only to particular memberships. Thankfully, this is a very easy step, and only takes a short time to set up.

Create test accounts, so you can make sure that users can view your content with the correct membership.

1 Open up a page you have already created

2 On the right hand side, you will see a box which will allow you to select the appropriate membership

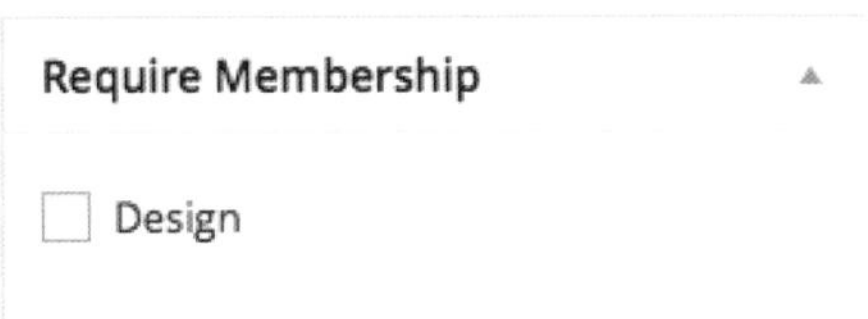

3 Tick the box for that particular membership. In the example above, you would tick the box called Design, as you only want Design members to access the page

4 Update or Publish the page. This will make sure that only those particular members can access that page

...cont'd

Page Settings

You now need to create and assign various WordPress pages for your Paid Membership Pro pages. These are things like account pages where the user can edit their details, checkout pages for paid membership, a page where the user can cancel their account plus many more. The plugin can automatically create these pages for you, and automatically assign them.

1. Go to **Memberships > Page Settings** from the Dashboard

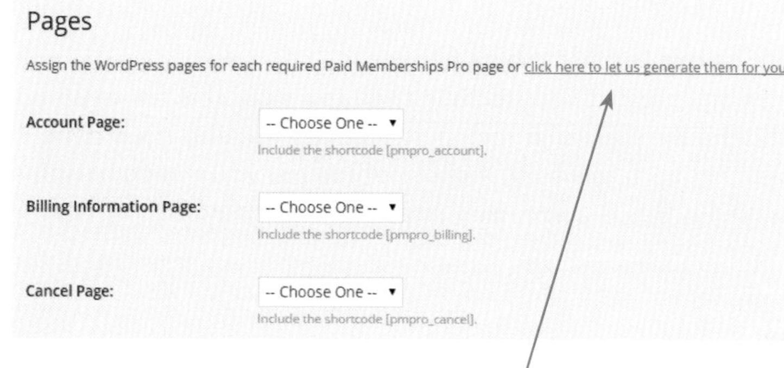

2. Select **Click here to let us generate them for you** at the top of the page. This will automatically set up the necessary pages

If you go to your live website, there should be an option called **Membership Account** in the main menu. This is a page that was automatically generated by Paid Memberships Pro. This is where the user can sign up for any of the memberships you created.

If the membership account page is not in your menu, be sure to add it yourself. See page 37 for how to add pages to the menu.

On the Membership Account page, the user then select which membership level they wish to sign up for.

Level	Price	
Design	Free	Select

← Return to Home

The user can then fill out the fields to sign up. If they already have an account they can also choose to sign in.

Membership Level *change*

You have selected the Design membership level.

Some design membership

The price for membership is $0.00 now.

Account Information *Already have an account? Log in here.*

Username *

Password *

Confirm Password *

E-mail Address *

Confirm E-mail Address *

Submit and Confirm »

The user can then view their account by selecting that same **Membership Account** link in their menu. This will allow them to change their current membership, change their passwords and view invoices if they have paid for membership.

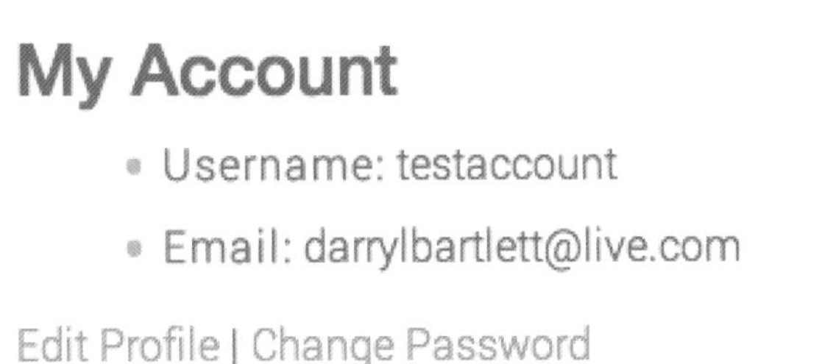

When the user signs up for a membership, they will automatically get a welcome email.

...cont'd

Payment Settings

If you wish to receive payments for membership, then you will need configure the payment settings.

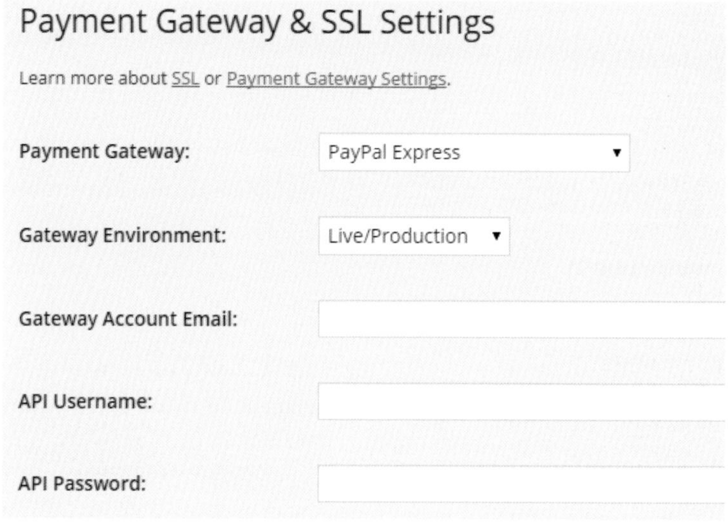

You will need to set the Gateway Environment to Live/Production, or all transactions will be test payments.

To set up your payment options:

1. Go to **Memberships** > **Payment Settings** from the Dashboard

The set up options will depend on which payment methods you decide to accept. PayPal is usually the best choice for online payments. You will need to set up your API details (API Username, API Password, API Signature by going to the PayPal developer website: **https://developer.paypal.com**

Email Settings

1. Go to **Memberships** > **Email Settings** from the Dashboard

This section is self explanatory. It will set up various email settings – for example, you may want to recieve a new email when a user cancels their account or when the user changes their membership level.

10 Tips & Tricks

This chapter will take you through some of the techniques to enhance your WordPress websites even further.

Google Analytics

Google Analytics is a great way of gaining detailed statistics about your website visitors. This could be extremely useful, especially if you want to find out how many daily visitors you are getting, or to monitor where the visitors to your site are coming from.

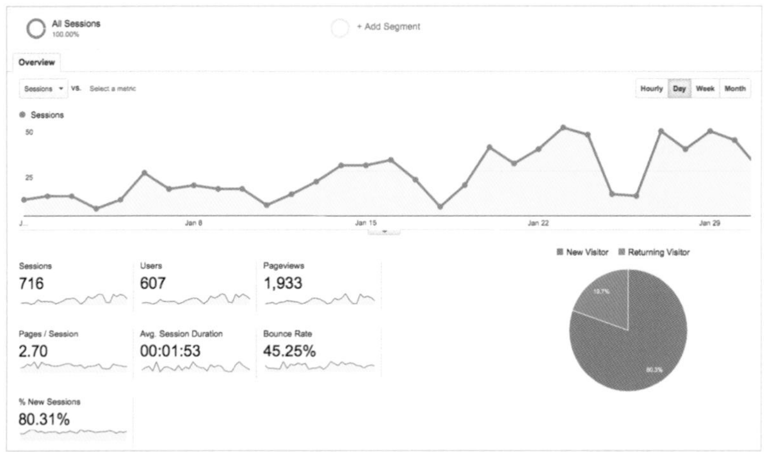

What Google Analytics Can Tell Me

- How many visitors your website has had (hourly, daily, weekly, and monthly)
- Where your visitors are coming from
- Web browsers that your visitors are using
- Keywords used by your visitors in search engines to get to your website

Signing up for Google Analytics

First of all, you need to sign up to Google Analytics.

1. Go to **www.google.com/analytics/**
2. During signup, you will be asked to enter the website name and URL – this is the one you want to track. Then click **Get Tracking ID**

Get Tracking ID Cancel

You will be given a code that you can enter into pages on your website.

This is your tracking code. Copy and pas

```
<script>
  (function(i,s,o,g,r,a,m){i['GoogleAnalyticsObject']=r;i[
  (i[r].q=i[r].q||[]).push(arguments)},i[r].l=1*new Date();
  m=s.getElementsByTagName(o)[0];a.async=1;a.src
  })(window,document,'script','//www.google-analytics.

  ga('create',            'auto');
  ga('send', 'pageview');

</script>
```

Google Analytics is a key tool for businesses, as it can show you where your customers are coming from and even tell you which marketing strategies are working out the best.

To get Google Analytics on to your WordPress website, so you can start gaining valuable statistics:

1. Copy your code from the screen above
2. From your Dashboard go to **Appearance > Editor**
3. Select **Header.php** from the right hand side. The code window will now display header.php on the left hand side
4. Place the Google Analytics code that you just copied directly below the <body> tag

```
        <meta charset="<?php bloginfo( 'charset' ); ?>">
        <meta name="viewport" content="width=device-width
        <title><?php wp_title( '|', true, 'right' ); ?></
        <link rel="profile" href="http://gmpg.org/xfn/11"
        <link rel="pingback" href="<?php bloginfo( 'pingb
        <!--[if lt IE 9]>
        <script src="<?php echo get_template_directory_ur
        <![endif]-->
        <?php wp_head(); ?>
</head>

<body <?php body_class(); ?>>
|
<div id="page" class="hfeed site">
        <?php if ( get_header_image() ) : ?>
        <div id="site-header">
```

Below <body> tag

5. Click **Save Changes**. Analytics will now start tracking activity. It will take 24 hours before your Google Analytics Dashboard will display any activity

Online Marketing for Small Businesses in easy steps covers the key tools at your disposal for online marketing.

Google Maps

Google Maps is useful if you want to show where your business is located. WP Google Maps is a free plugin and gives many options for your map.

Google Maps is ideal for your contact page. It can show your exact location to potential customers.

1. Go to **Plugins** > **Add New**
2. Type in WP Google Maps and click **Search Plugins**

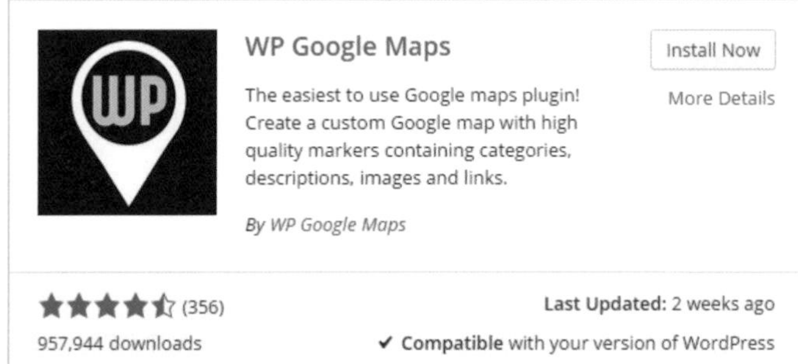

3. Click **Install Now** under WP Google Maps. Don't forget to activate it once it's been installed

You should see an option called **Maps** on the left hand side of the Dashboard.

4. Click **Maps** > **Maps**

There should be one map already created called **My first map**. This is where your list of maps will appear.

5. Click on **My first map**, or the **Edit** button. Both will take you to that map

ID	Title
1	**My first map** Edit

...cont'd

General Settings | Directions | Store Locator | Advanced Settings | **Pro Upgrade**

Short code: [wpgmza id="1"] *copy this into your post or page to display the map*
Map Name: My first map
Width: 100 % *Set to 100% for a responsive map*
Height: 400 px
Zoom Level:
Map Alignment: Left
Map type: Roadmap

From here you will be presented with some map options:

Shortcode: Leave this! This is what you will copy and paste into your post or page to display the map.

Map Name: Choose a name for the map.

Width/Height: Here you can set your map height and width.

Zoom Level: Select how far you want the map to be zoomed in. A preview will appear at the bottom right hand side.

Map Alignment: Left, Center or Right.

Map Type: Here you can select whether or not the map displays the road, satellite image, hybrid or terrain views.

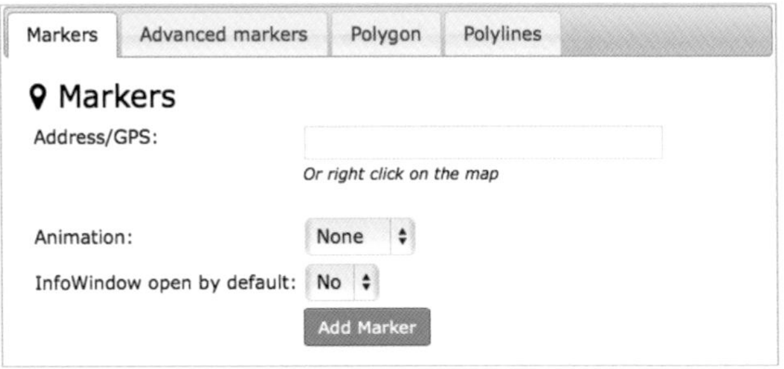

6. Enter the address where you want your marker to be placed. Then click **Add Marker**. The preview should update

7. Finally, save your map. You can now add this shortcode to your post or page

Paragraph
[wpgmza id="1"]

Using CSS

Using CSS is a great way to alter the way your website looks. You can change text, images, website structure etc. All WordPress websites use CSS, so if you really want to enhance your website, then this is a great tool. Let's have a look at ways that CSS can help you.

Hot tip

CSS is a style language that defines the layout of web pages. It covers things like fonts, colors, margins, backgrounds, widths etc.

1. First, download or open the Google Chrome web browser (**www.google.com/chrome**)

2. Go to your WordPress website and right click on one of your elements – in this case, a post title. Then click on **Inspect element** from the dropdown list

You will see a bar appear at the bottom or side of your page, which looks something like the one shown below

Do not mess with CSS unless you know what you're doing.

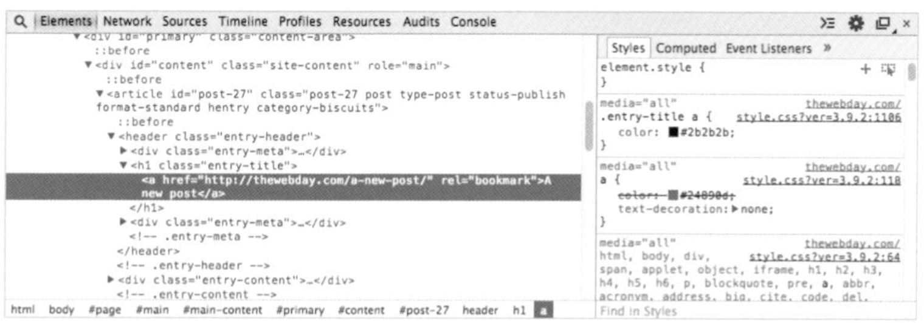

Using the Inspect Element tool is a great way of understanding CSS. It's also a good way to tweak the code to see how it will work before adding it to the style sheet.

The box on the right hand side or at the bottom displays attributes for that particular element. In this case it's the title for one of the posts. This element is called **.entry-title a.**

```
media="all"                    thewebday.com/
.entry-title a {    style.css?ver=3.9.2:1106
   color: ■#2b2b2b;
}
```

You can change the code here to get a preview of what the website would look like if you were to change the CSS code.

Change the text colour to red and change the font size to 38px by clicking in the element inspector and adding the following lines.

color: red;
font-size: 38px;

```
media="all"                        thewebday.com/
.entry-title a {    style.css?ver=3.9.2:1106
   color: ■red;
   font-size: 38px;
}
```

You will now notice that the live website provides a preview of how it looks. So the text now looks like this:

HELLO WORLD!

This is only a preview and doesn't change the live site. To do this, you need to go into the Editor and change the code from there.

1. Go to **Appearance > Editor**
2. Select **Stylesheet (style.css)** from the right hand side

Styles
Stylesheet
(style.css)
RTL Stylesheet
(rtl.css)

```
.entry-title {
        font-size: 33px;
        font-weight: 300;
        line-height: 1.0909090909;
        margin-bottom: 12px;
        margin: 0 0 12px 0;
        text-transform: uppercase;
}

.entry-title a {
        color: #2b2b2b;
}

.entry-title a:hover {
        color: #41a62a;
}
```

The code for the stylesheet will now appear on the left hand side. You need to find the element name. In this case, look for **.entry-title a**

Your elements will all have different names. It all depends what the Theme developer has named them.

Developing your skills in CSS is a fantastic way to enhance your website. It is key if you are looking to start out as a developer.

Why not try out CSS3 in easy steps to learn more about CSS.

...cont'd

3. Now, type in the changes you want to make. When you have finished, click **Update File** and the changes will appear live on your website

```
        font-weight: 300;
        line-height: 1.0909090909;
        margin-bottom: 12px;
        margin: 0 0 12px 0;
        text-transform: uppercase;
}

.entry-title a {
        color: red;
        font-size: 38px;
}

.entry-title a:hover {
        color: #41a62a;
}
```

Element Code

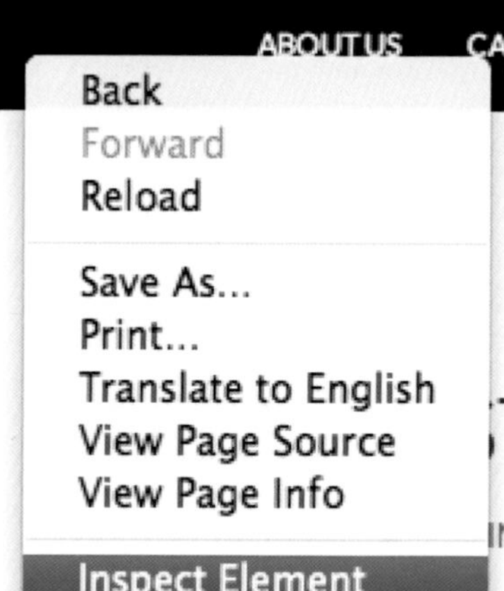

Let's try one more example.

4. Right click on the header menu on the website and click **Inspect Element**

Once again the menu will appear at the bottom of the page, along with the selected element on the right hand side

```
.header-main {      style.css?ver=3.9.2:3352

}
```

5. To make the menu colour green, you would add the code **background-color: green;** to the element, as shown below:

.header-main {
background-color: green;
}

ABOUT US CART CHECKOUT CONTACT US

The website preview in the browser has changed – it is now green.

Next, go back to **Appearance > Editor** and change the code for that element in the stylesheet (style.css) file.

There is a lot more to CSS than this. You can change all kinds of elements but it really helps you to understand the design.

Some basic samples of CSS code

Below are some samples of CSS and their meanings. You can try them out on your own elements.

text-transform: uppercase;
This code will transform the text into uppercase. For example if your text was "hello", then it would be changed to "HELLO".

border-bottom: thick dotted black;
This code will add a black dotted border at the bottom of the element. You can use border-top, border-left etc. too.

float: left;
Using the float element will specify if the box floats to the left or the right. In this instance it's to the left. You can also choose "none" which means the box will not float.

padding-right: 50px;
Padding will clear the area around that particular element. In this instance it will add a 50px area to the right of the element. You can also use padding-left, padding-top etc.

background-image: url("biscuit.gif");
You can add background images using the code above. The image is usually repeated by default until the element is covered.

font-family: "Times New Roman", Georgia, Serif;
This will specify the font for a particular element. If the first font is not available, it will use the next one in the list.

Newsletter Forms

MailChimp is a very simple tool to use to create email campaigns. It does not require any coding knowledge and integrates nicely into WordPress.

If you'd like to send out a newsletter by email to your readers or customers, then adding a newsletter sign up form to your website is a really good idea. Any new readers that visit your website can then easily sign up. Sending out newsletters is a good way of keeping visitors coming back to your website. MailChimp is a really good way to create and distribute newsletters and you don't need to have any technical knowledge.

To create a signup form on your website, so that every time someone subscribes it will add them to one of your MailChimp lists:

1. Create a MailChimp account if you don't already have one. You can sign up at **www.mailchimp.com**

Get Started with a Free Account

Sign up in 30 seconds. No credit card required. If you already have a MailChimp account, log in.

2. Go to **Plugins** > **Install New** and search for **Easy MailChimp Forms**

Easy MailChimp Forms

Install Now

More Details

Easy MailChimp Forms allows you to painlessly add MailChimp sign up forms to your WordPress site and track user activity with interactive reports.

By YIKES Inc

96,664 downloads

Last Updated: 4 weeks ago

✔ **Compatible** with your version of WordPress

3. Install and Activate the plugin

Configuring Easy MailChimp Forms

You will notice a new link on the left hand side of the Dashboard called **MailChimp Forms**.

1. Click **MailChimp Forms > MailChimp Settings**

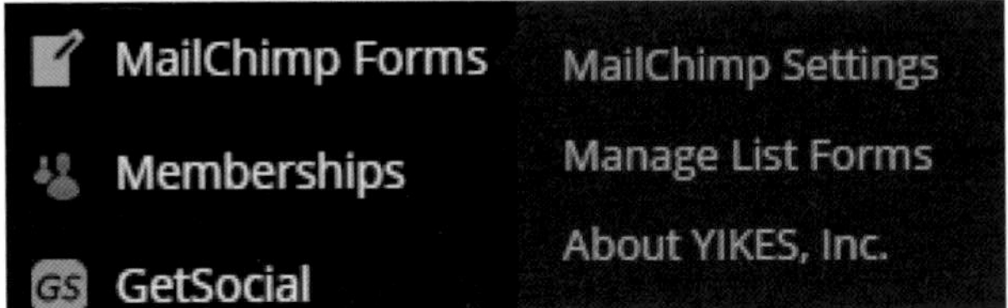

2. Configure the various options to get started

Easy Mailchimp Forms by YIKES, Inc.
Manage Mailchimp Forms Settings
Your Mailchimp API Key
Please enter your MailChimp API
For more help, visit the MailChim
Preferred Form Layout
div
Choose whether you want your f

Your MailChimp API Key: You can get hold of this from your MailChimp account.

3. Log in to MailChimp. Click your name on the left hand side and select **Account**

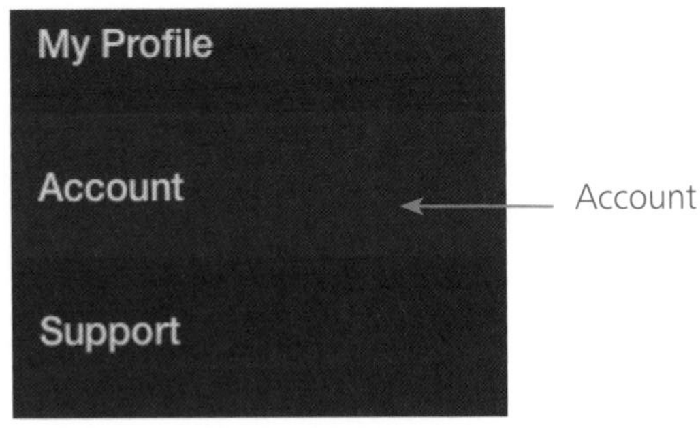

...cont'd

4. Click **Extras** along the top bar and then select **API Keys**

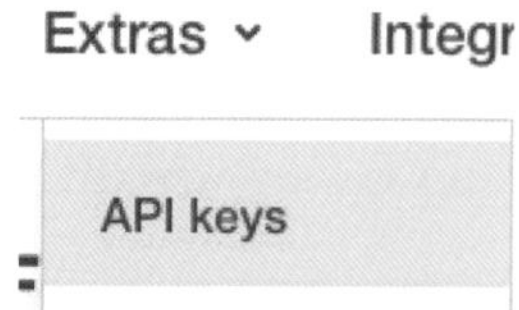

5. Click **Create A Key** under **Your API Keys**

6. Finally, copy your API key from the field

7. Head back to your MailChimp Settings in the Dashboard. Paste your code into the **Your MailChimp API Key**. It should come up with a tickbox to confirm it's a valid key

8. Click **Save Settings** at the bottom of the page

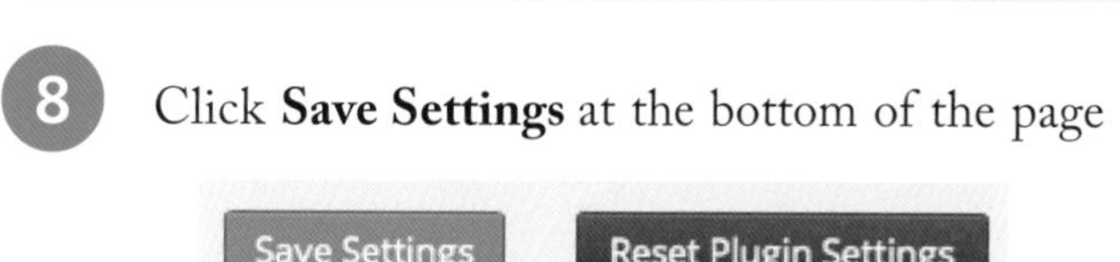

Adding MailChimp Forms

You are now almost ready to start creating forms for your website. First of all, you need to create a list in MailChimp, so that when users visit your website and fill out their details, they will be added to your newsletter list.

1. Log in to MailChimp and select **Lists** from the left hand side of the page

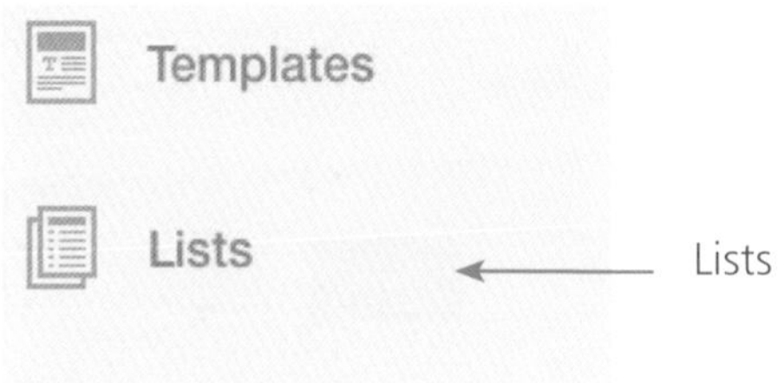

Lists

2. Select **Create List** from the top right

Create List

3. Create your list

Lists
Create List

List details

List name

Default "from" email

List Name: This can be anything you like. Your subscribers will see this when they sign up.

Default "from" Email: This is the email that your subscribers will reply to.

Default "from" Name: When users recieve your newsletter, this is the name they will see. Use something like your company name.

Reminder: You will need to write a short sentence here to remind users how they got on your list. In this case, it will be because they subscribed through the website.

Contact Information: This is likely to already be filled out. It will contain your company details.

In your newsletter campaigns, remember to only use email addresses from customers who have signed up via the website, or who have given you permission.

...cont'd

4 Next, click **Save**

5 Now, from your WordPress Dashboard, go to **MailChimp Forms > Manage List Forms**

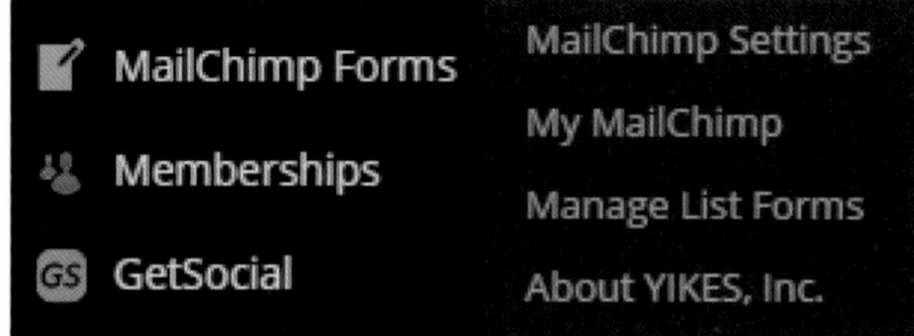

6 Select your List from the dropdown box and click **Create a Form for this List**

The shortcode is created, you will use this in your page or post. Make sure you copy it down.

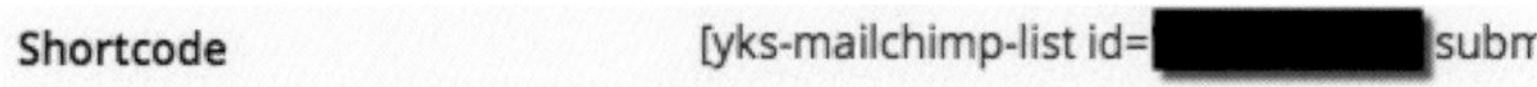

There are a couple of other options, like selecting which fields to add to the form and you can choose to direct our user to another web page after signing up.

7 Click **Save Settings** at the bottom of the page. You are now ready to add your shortcode to your pages

8. Finally, open up the page you wish to add the form to and paste it into the Visual Editor.

Email Address *

First Name

Last Name

Submit

Your form should now be live on your website. Now, every time a user signs up, their email address will be added to your list, ready for when you create an email campaign with MailChimp.

You won't be able to manage your lists from within WordPress. You will have to go to the MailChimp website to manage your subscribers.

Comment Box Opt-In

You also have the choice to add a opt-in checkbox on comment forms, so that when users are commenting on your content, a tickbox will appear asking them if they want to sign up to the newsletter.

1. Go to **Mailchimp Forms** > **MailChimp Settings** from the Dashboard

2. Scroll down until you find **Display opt-in checkbox on comment forms?** and change the dropdown box to **Show**

Display opt-in checkbox on comment forms? Show

3. Select the Default List and enter some Comment Checkbox Text, then click **Save Settings**

Now the option will appear for your visitors to be able to opt-in to the newsletter when they are commenting on the content on your website.

...cont'd

Single or Double Opt-In

If you go to **MailChimp Forms > MailChimp Settings** from the Dashboard you can also choose whether or not you want a Single or Double Opt-In. A Single Opt-In is when the user signs up via the form, and it doesn't require them to verify their subscription by email. A Double Opt-In will will send out an email to the user asking them to verify their email address.

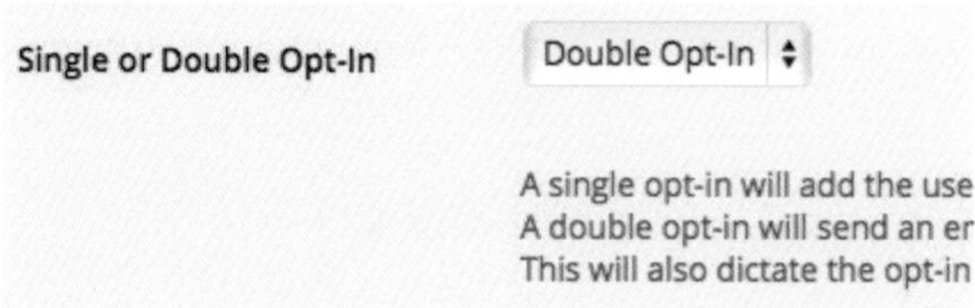

Custom Opt-In Message

This can also be set in **MailChimp Forms > MailChimp Settings**. It allows you to create a custom message to display once the user has signed up for the newsletter.

Don't force users to sign up. Try to explain the benefits of signing up for your newsletter. Sometimes adding an incentive can help.

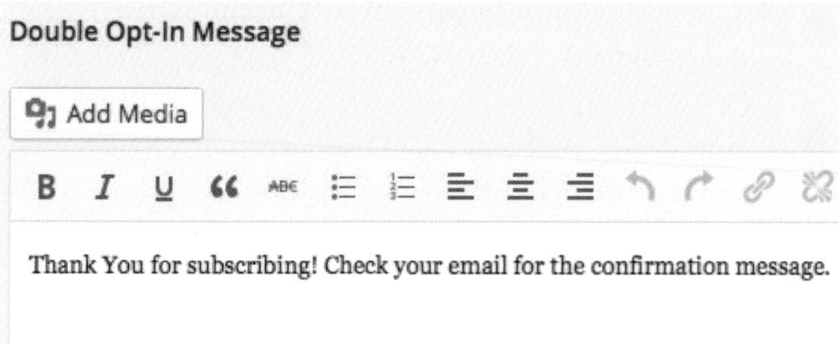

Having a newsletter is a great way to keep in touch with your website users. Remember to send out a regular newsletter with a teaser of your content, and then add links in it to the content on your website. This will build a relationship with your readers and keep them coming back to your website.

Sitemaps

A sitemap lists all the pages of your website. It can tell search engines about the organization of your site content, and when new or existing pages are updated and available for crawling. There is a good plugin called Google XML Sitemaps that generates an XML sitemap.

1. Go to **Plugins** > **Add New**

2. Type in Google XML Sitemaps and click **Search Plugins**

Google XML Sitemaps

This plugin will generate a special XML sitemap which will help search engines to better index your blog.

By Arne Brachhold

3. Install and activate the plugin

4. The sitemap.xml will automatically be created. However, you can customize the settings by going to **Settings** > **XML-Sitemap**

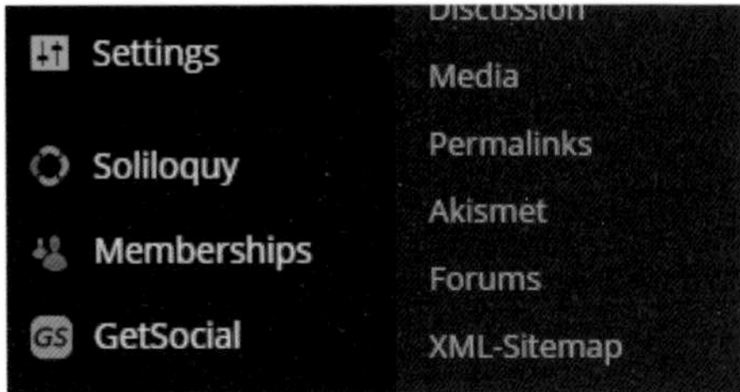

5. Your sitemap will now be live. There are some optional settings that you might wish to change

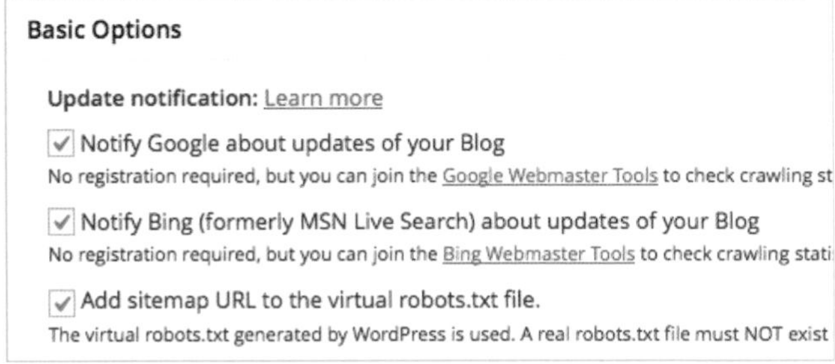

...cont'd

Pinging is used to notify various online search engines that a blog/website has been updated. Typically, a search engine will follow links and index the new post quicker as a result.

A crawler is a program that most search engines use to find what's new on the Internet. It basically crawls the web and collects documents to build a searchable index for the different search engines. The program starts at a website and follows every hyperlink on each page.

Update Notification

Notify Google about updates of your Blog: Google will be notified every time content is updated or added.

Notify Bing about updates of your Blog: Bing (formerly MSN Live Search) will be notified every time content is updated or added.

Add sitemap URL to the virtual robots.txt file: This will allow search engines that don't support ping to find your sitemap.

Advanced Options

Most of these options you don't need to worry about. Make sure that **Include Sitemap in HTML format** is ticked, as an HTML sitemap allows site visitors to easily navigate a website. It is basically a text version of your site navigation.

Additional Pages

Here you specify pages which should be included in your sitemap, but may not belong to to your blog or website. For example, if your domain is *www.biscuit.com* and your blog is located on *www.biscuit.com/blog* then you might want to include your homepage www.biscuit.com.

Post Priority

In this section you can specify how the priority of each post will be calculated. Posts with high priority values are likely to get indexed faster and crawled more often. You can set them to have the same priority, use the number of comments, or use the comment average.

Sitemap Content

Here you can select what you want to include in your sitemap. The homepage, posts and pages will be automatically selected. You can, however, add things like categories, author pages and archives.

Excluded Items

You can choose to exclude particular posts, pages and categories from your sitemap. Just select the categories or type the posts or pages you want to exclude.

Change Frequencies & Priorities

You can give an indication to search engines of how often content changes on your website, and finally you are able to give the search engines an indication of the priorities of your page types.

Google Fonts

In the early days of the web, the Internet was filled with boring standard fonts, mainly because developers were limited to using fonts commonly found on most computers. These days, developers have a lot of choice thanks to web fonts. Google Fonts is just one way you can change the fonts on your website without the user having to have the font already stored on their computer.

Getting Started with Google Fonts

Before you get Google Fonts set up on your WordPress website, we are going to have a look at how you can discover great fonts on the Google Fonts website. Let's begin by going to **https://www.google.com/fonts**

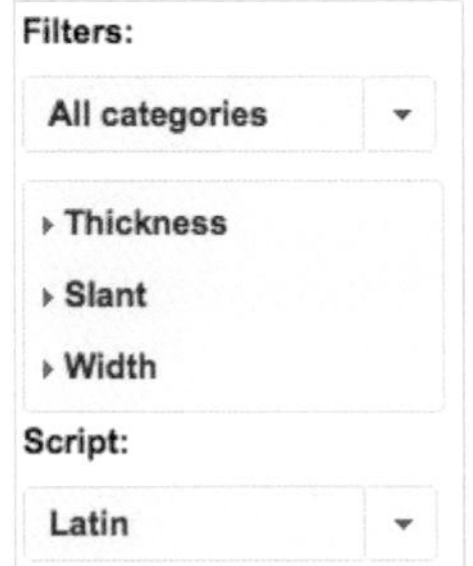

You will notice a number of filters along the left hand side, that will help you find the type of font you are looking for

Different fonts will appear down the center of the page.

You don't have to download the fonts to use them on your website.

You can even preview your text by entering text into the **Preview Text** box.

Preview Text: Grumpy wizards make toxic brew

Using WP Google Fonts

There is a great plugin you can use called WP Google Fonts which is especially helpful for beginners, if you don't want to get involved with adding code.

...cont'd

1. Go to **Plugins** > **Add New** from the WordPress Dashboard

2. Search for **WP Google Fonts** in the search bar, and Install and then Activate

WP Google Fonts

The WP Google Fonts plugin allows you to easily add fonts from the Google Font Directory to your Wordpress theme.

By Adrian Hanft, Aaron Brown

3. Now head to **Settings** > **Google Fonts** from the Dashboard

A font selection page will appear, which allows you to choose six different fonts for your website. You can add one font to each of the six dropdown boxes.

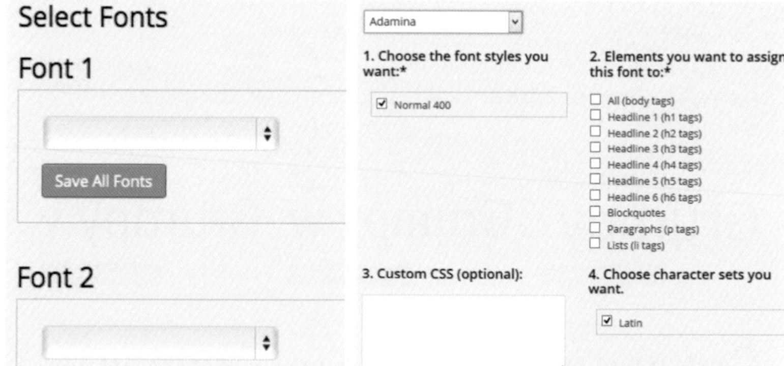

Font Selection | Font Options

1. Choose the font styles you want to use: Some fonts will have their own different styles, for example "Regular" or "Bold".
2. Elements you want to assign this font to: Here you select the elements you want to assign the font to. You might want to assign it to header 1, or the main paragraph text.
3. Custom CSS (optional): You can add your own custom CSS.
4. Choose character sets you want: Make sure you select any character sets you want.
5. Save All Fonts: Saves the changes to all font selections.

Save All Fonts

Check out the previews of your font on the Google Fonts website, so that you know how your font will look.

Save your changes so that your elements will update straight away with the new font choices.

11 Advanced WordPress

This final chapter covers more advanced topics like setting up FTP, website backups, creating a theme, and responsive design.

WordPress & PHP

PHP is the server-side web development language behind WordPress. You don't need to know PHP to use WordPress. However, it is a good way to add extra functionality or enhance your website even further. It also comes in handy if you want to develop your own themes or plugins. We will show you how to create your own theme on page 166.

WordPress Theme Files

A WordPress theme consists of several files. These are the basic ones that are the key fundamentals behind the main website:

- **index.php** – This file usually sets up the homepage unless there is a home.php file. This file can also be used to generate other pages. For example, if WordPress cannot find the file specific to that page, then it will use the index file.
- **header.php** – This file controls the header. Most of your pages will share the same header.
- **footer.php** – This file controls the footer (at the very bottom of the page). Footers are great for adding copyright notices etc.
- **siderbar.php** – This file controls all the sidebar content.
- **single.php** – This file will set up all single page posts on your blog or website.
- **page.php** – This file will control all your pages.
- **archive.php** – This file will control the layout of the achive pages. For example, you may have a page in a "June 2010" category.
- **style.css** - This controls the styling for your website. For example, your layout, look, elements and colors, etc.

You will find all these files in your WordPress Editor by going to **Appearance** > **Editor** from the Dashboard.

Setting up FTP

FTP (File Transfer Protocol) allows you to move files from your computer to your hosting account in a quick and simple manner. Most web developers will use FTP as they can transfer lots of files, and it allows them to manage their website just by using an FTP client. An FTP client, such as FileZilla, is a piece of downloadable software that allows you to easily move files from your computer to a web host or another computer. To get FTP set up you will need to do two things:

FTP is a much quicker way to move files from your computer to your hosting account.

Set up an FTP Account with HostGator

The first thing we need to do is setup an FTP account. The process is very similar with most hosting companies, and a lot of web hosts will provide documentation on their website. If you are using HostGator then follow these steps to set up your FTP account:

1. Log in to your HostGator Control Panel, just like you did in Chapter 1 (see page 12)
2. Scroll down to Files and click **FTP Accounts**

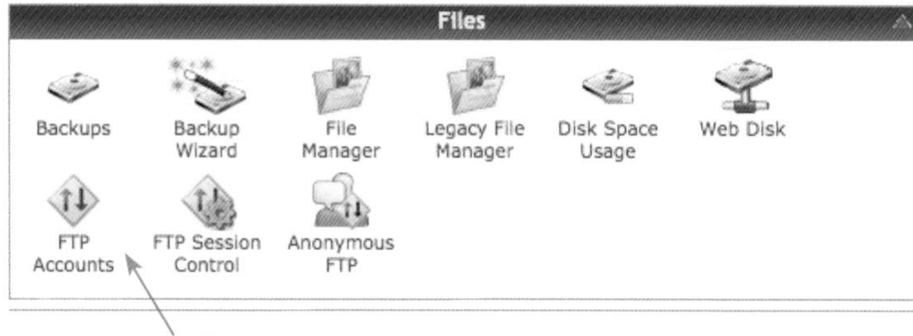

FTP Accounts

3. Complete the form:

   Login: Choose a login name. This will eventually be login@yourdomain.com

   Password: Enter a password for the account

   Password Again: Re-enter the password

   Directory: Make sure this ends with public_html as shown in the screenshot on the next page

   Quota: Set a quota for the FTP account

...cont'd

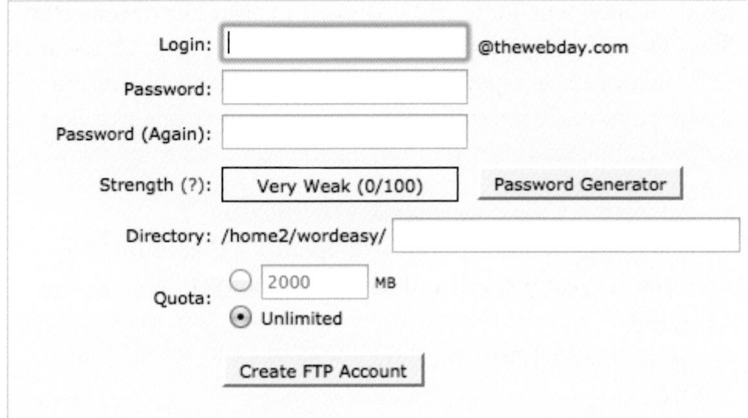

4. Now all you need to do is click **Create FTP Account** and you're ready to go

Download and configure an FTP Client called FileZilla

You will need an FTP client to access your files. FileZilla is a great choice.

1. Download it at: **https://filezilla-project.org**
2. Open up the application

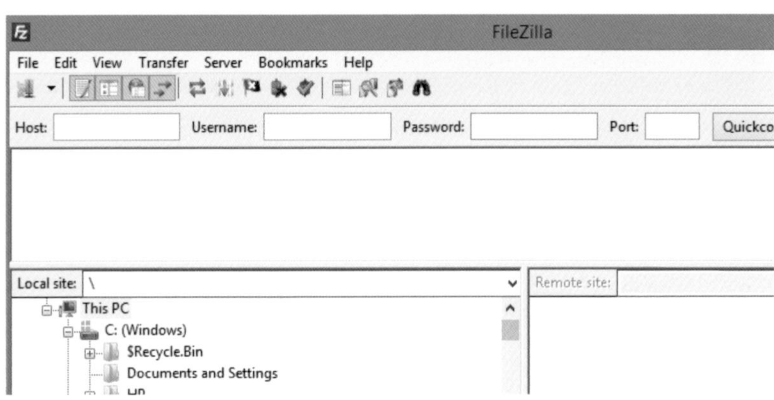

At the top of the application there is a bar with a number of fields you need to fill out.

3. Enter your Host (ftp.yourdomain.com), Username (the one you set up under FTP accounts), and your password. Now click **QuickConnect**

If the status reads **Directory Listing Successful** then you are connected.

```
Response:     150 Accepted data connection
Response:     226-Options: -a -l
Response:     226 23 matches total
Status:       Directory listing successful
```

The window on the right will display all your hosting files. The window on the left will display all the files on your computer. If you wish to upload a file from your computer, all you need to do is drag the file from the left window (Computer) to the right window (Hosting Files).

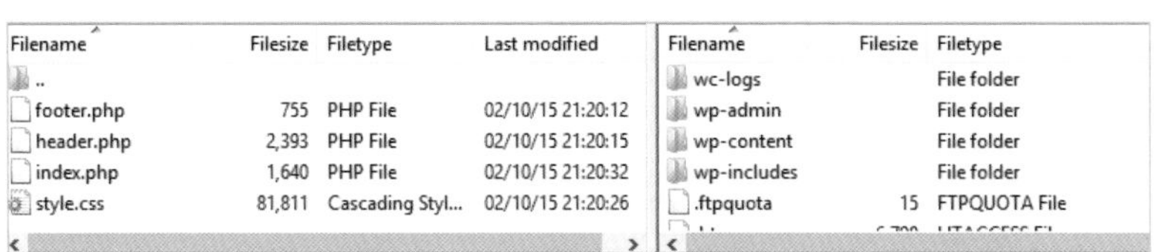

Left Window (Computer Files)   Right Window (Host Files)

If you are looking to edit PHP files, or the stylesheet for the theme you currently have activated, then in the right FileZilla window navigate to **wp-content > themes > themename.** You can find your theme name in the Dashboard by going to **Apperance > Themes**

You should now see your theme files (header.php, footer.php, and style.css etc.) You can double click them to open right there. However, it is advised to drag a copy to your computer to edit.

Make sure you keep a backup of your files.

Depending on your broadband connection, it can take some time to transfer files.

Creating a Theme

Earlier in the book you were shown how to add and upload themes. Now we will show you how to create a basic one. This should help you gain a better knowledge of HTML and PHP, and will help create better websites.

Remember the PHP files that we talked about on page 162 that make up a WordPress theme? We will show you how to create five of them to make up our theme.

- **index.php**
- **header.php**
- **footer.php**
- **sider.php**
- **style.css**

Text Editor

You are going to need a text editor to create these files, something like Notepad, or you can use a professional code editor like Sublime Text.

Remember to use a text editor that you are comfortable with. It may take some time to familarize yourself with the layout.

Index File (index.php)

1. Open up your text editor and enter the following code:

```
<?php get_header(); ?>
<div id="main">
<div id="content">
<?php if (have_posts()) : while (have_posts()) : the_post(); ?>
<h1><?php the_title(); ?></h1>
<h4>Posted on <?php the_time('F jS, Y') ?></h4>
<p><?php the_content(__('(more...)')); ?></p>
<hr> <?php endwhile; else: ?>
<p><?php _e('Sorry, there are no posts available at this time.');
?></p><?php endif; ?>
</div>
<?php get_sidebar(); ?>
</div>
<div id="delimiter">
</div>
<?php get_footer(); ?>
```

```
index.php
<?php get_header(); ?>
<div id="main">
<div id="content">
<?php if (have_posts()) : while (have_posts()) : the_post(); ?>
<h1><?php the_title(); ?></h1>
<h4>Posted on <?php the_time('F jS, Y') ?></h4>
<p><?php the_content(__('(more...)')); ?></p>
<hr> <?php endwhile; else: ?>
<p><?php _e('Sorry, there are no posts available at this time.');
?></p><?php endif; ?>
</div>
<?php get_sidebar(); ?>
</div>
<div id="delimiter">
</div>
<?php get_footer(); ?>
```

2. Make sure you save your file as index.php

Index File Explained

<?php get_header(); ?>
This will grab the header and include it in this page. As mentioned before, the header is used in all pages on a website.

<?php if (have_posts()) : while (have_posts()) : the_post(); ?>
<h1><?php the_title(); ?></h1>
<h4>Posted on <?php the_time('F jS, Y') ?></h4>
<p><?php the_content(__('(more...)')); ?></p>
<hr> <?php endwhile; else: ?>
<p><?php _e('Sorry, there are no posts available at this time.');
?></p><?php endif; ?>

This will bring in the posts on your website. As you can see, it brings in the title, time posted and the content of the post. If there are no posts on the website, then it will leave a message saying "Sorry there are no posts available at this time." If you set your homepage to display a static page, then that content will appear there instead.

<?php get_sidebar(); ?>
Bring in the sidebar code and get this inserted into your page.

<?php get_footer(); ?>
Finally, bring in the footer. This is the last thing you will bring in to your page.

There are a number of online resources to help you learn to code. The Code Academy (**www.codeacademy.com**) is one of the better ones out there.

PHP & MySQL in easy steps will teach you how to write PHP server-side scripts.

...cont'd

Header File

Create a new file in your text editor and enter the following:

```
<html>
<head>
<title>My Page Title</title>
<link rel="stylesheet" href="<?php bloginfo('stylesheet_url');
?>">
</head>
<body>
<div id="wrapper">
<div id="header">
<h1>Some Title for the Top</h1>
</div>
```

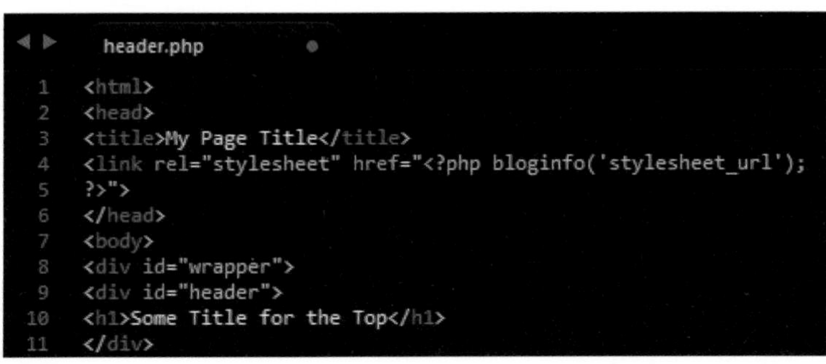

The header.php file will be used throughout all of your WordPress web pages.

Save the file as header.php

A <div id> is used to identify a single element that only appears once, a bit like a header. A <div class> tag is used to identify elements that are used more than once. For example, a widget or an image area.

Header File Explained

```
<title>My Page Title</title>
```

This will assign a title to the website at the top of the browser.

```
<link rel="stylesheet" href="<?php bloginfo('stylesheet_url');
?>">
```

This tells WordPress to load the style.css file.

```
<div id="wrapper">
<div id="header">
```

Notice how you have created some div tags here. We will later go on to style these in our style.css file.

A <div> tag is used to specify a section within an HTML document.

<h1>Some Title for the Top</h1>
We have added a title in your header saying "Some Title for the Top", but you can come up with something creative. This is styled using <h1>, which is Header 1.

Footer File

1. Create a new file in your text editor and enter the following:

```
<div id="footer">
<h1>This is our footer</h1>
<a href="http://www.thewebday.com">Web Day</a>
</div>
</div>
</body>
</html>
```

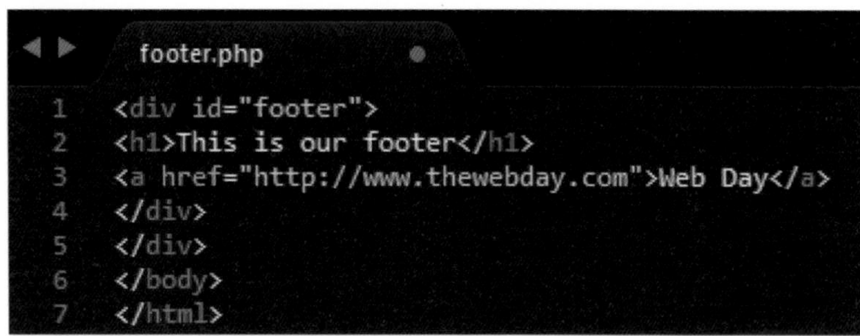

The footer is a good place for things like copyright notices.

2. Save the file as footer.php

Footer File Explained

<div id="footer">
Here we create a div that we can use in the stylesheet (style.css) later on.

<h1>This is our footer</h1>
We are going to add a title to our footer; we may not usually do this when it comes to developing websites.

...cont'd

It is important to add the extension .php at the end of your files when saving.

In this scenario, we have specified the title to point out the footer.

<a href="http://www.thewebday.com">Web Day</a>
This will add a link in the footer. The first part specifes the actual link of the website, and the last part is how the actual link will appear on the page.

Sidebar File

1. Create a new file in your text editor and enter the following:

```
<div id="sidebar">
<h2 ><?php _e('Categories'); ?></h2>
<ul >
<?php wp_list_cats('sort_column=name&optioncount=1&hiera
rchical=0'); ?>
</ul>
<h2 ><?php _e('Archives'); ?></h2>
<ul >
<?php wp_get_archives('type=monthly'); ?>
</ul>
</div>
```


```
sidebar.php
<div id="sidebar">
<h2 ><?php _e('Categories'); ?></h2>
<ul >
<?php wp_list_cats('sort_column=name&optioncount=1&hiera
rchical=0'); ?>
</ul>
<h2 ><?php _e('Archives'); ?></h2>
<ul >
<?php wp_get_archives('type=monthly'); ?>
</ul>
</div>
```


2. Save the file as sidebar.php

In this example, the sidebar will appear on the right hand side. It is a great place to display a list of posts, or maybe even a list of your content categories.

Sidebar File Explained

Here we are looking to create links to our Categories and Archives, so let's break this down.

<div id="sidebar">
First we are setting up a div, so we can set this up in the stylesheet.

<h2 ><?php _e('Categories'); ?></h2>
This will show the word Categories in <h2> styling.

<?php wp_list_cats('sort_column=name&optioncount=1&hiera rchical=0'); ?>
This will set up our list of categories down the side of the page.

<h2 ><?php _e('Archives'); ?></h2>
This will set up another title saying Archives. This is styled using the <h2> attributes.

<?php wp_get_archives('type=monthly'); ?>
This will display our archives by month.

The stylesheet is a key element in styling the elements on your website.

Stylesheet File

Now we have the foundations set in place, we are going to begin setting up our elements.

Enter the following into a new file:

```
body { text-align: center; }
#wrapper { display: block; border: 1px #a2a2a2 solid; width:90%;
margin:0px auto; }
#header { border: 2px #a2a2a2 solid; background:red; }
#content { width: 75%; border: 5px #a2a2a2 solid; float: left;}
#sidebar { width: 23%; border: 2px #a2a2a2 solid; float: right; }
#delimiter { clear: both; }
#footer { border: 2px #a2a2a2 solid; }
.title { font-size: 11pt; font-family: verdana; font-weight: bold; }
h1 {font-size:40px;}
h2 {font-size:22px;}
p {font-size:14px;}
#footer h1 { font-size:35px;}
```

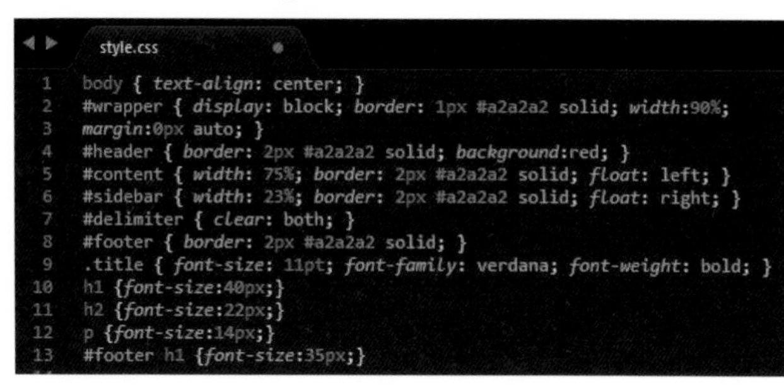

```
style.css
body { text-align: center; }
#wrapper { display: block; border: 1px #a2a2a2 solid; width:90%;
margin:0px auto; }
#header { border: 2px #a2a2a2 solid; background:red; }
#content { width: 75%; border: 2px #a2a2a2 solid; float: left; }
#sidebar { width: 23%; border: 2px #a2a2a2 solid; float: right; }
#delimiter { clear: both; }
#footer { border: 2px #a2a2a2 solid; }
.title { font-size: 11pt; font-family: verdana; font-weight: bold; }
h1 {font-size:40px;}
h2 {font-size:22px;}
p {font-size:14px;}
#footer h1 {font-size:35px;}
```

2. Save the file as style.css

Stylesheet File Explained

body { text-align: center; }
Here we are aligning all body content to the center.

#wrapper { display: block; border: 1px #a2a2a2 solid; width:90%; margin:0px auto; }
Here we are setting the details for our wrapper – this is where all our main content will go. We are setting this to a width of 90% and setting the border and margin attributes for it.

#header { border: 2px #a2a2a2 solid; background:red; }
Here we set the thickness and color of the border of the header. We are also setting the background of the header to red.

#sidebar { width: 23%; border: 2px #a2a2a2 solid; float: right; }
We are setting our sidebar to 23%, giving it a border and making sure the content floats to the right.

#footer { border: 2px #a2a2a2 solid; }
Here we set the thickness and color of the border for the footer.

.title { font-size: 11pt; font-family: verdana; font-weight: bold; }
h1 {font-size:40px;}
h2 {font-size:22px;}
p {font-size:14px;}
#footer h1 { font-size:35px;}
Here we are setting the font sizes for our headers and paragraphs. On page 170 we set up the heading "Categories" under <h2>. In this stylesheet we have set up h2 with a font size of 22px.

This is how our website will look once it goes live.

Uploading Files

Once you have finished writing and saving your files, you can upload them to your webspace.

1. Open up FileZilla

2. Enter your FTP details, as you created on page 163

3. Once you are logged in, find your theme files on your computer in the window on the left hand side

Filename	Filesize	Filetype
..		
footer.php	128	PHP File
header.php	212	PHP File
index.php	469	PHP File
sidebar.php	246	PHP File
style.css	537	Cascading Sty

4. In the right hand panel, navigate to **wp-content > themes.** In this folder, create your own folder, and name it. In this example, we have called it **mynewtheme**. Create a directory by right clicking in the window and selecting **Create directory**

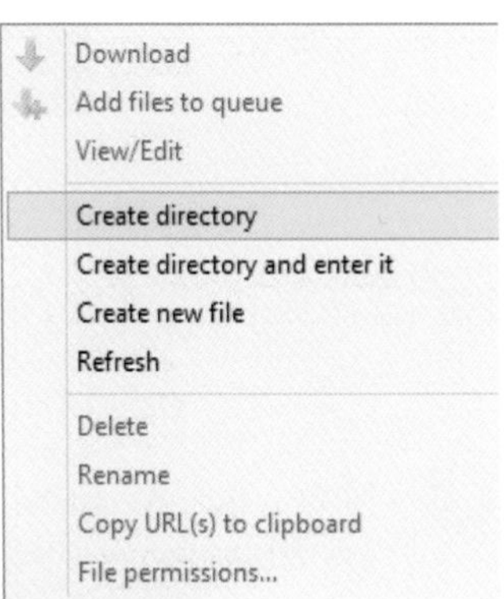

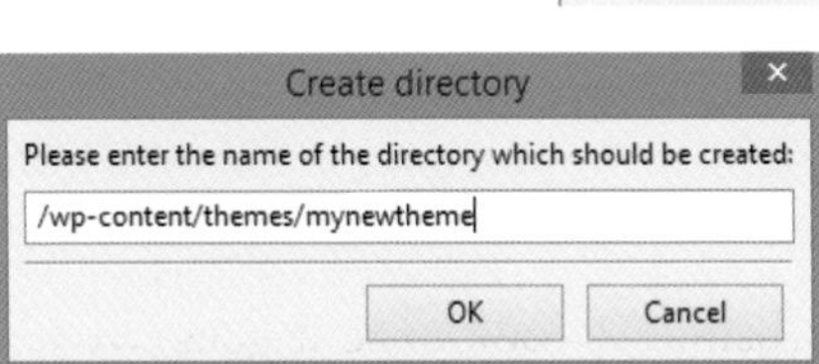

For now, make sure all your files are in the same directory to avoid errors.

...cont'd

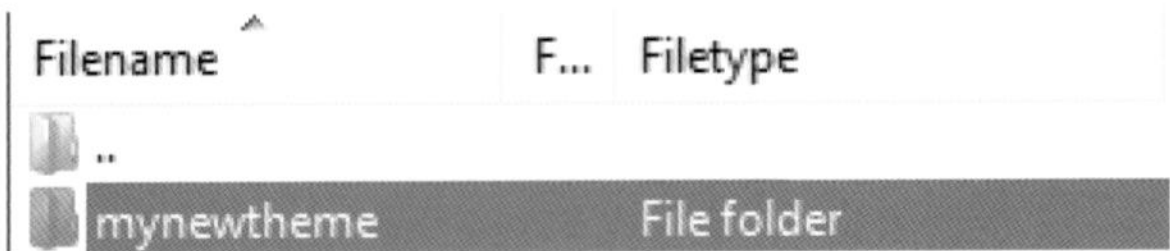

5. Once you have created the directory, double click it to open it. Now, drag across the files from the left window to the right to upload your files

Filename	Filesize	Filetype	Last modified
..			
footer.php	128	PHP File	02/10/15 22:09:34
header.php	212	PHP File	02/10/15 21:54:32
index.php	469	PHP File	02/10/15 21:49:33
sidebar.php	246	PHP File	02/10/15 22:33:39
style.css	537	Cascading Styl...	02/10/15 22:47:38

Left Window (Computer Files)

Filename	F...	Filetype
..		
Empty directory listing		

Right Window (Host Files)

6. You now need to activate your new theme in WordPress. Log in to the Dashboard and go to **Appearance > Themes.** You will notice your theme appears there

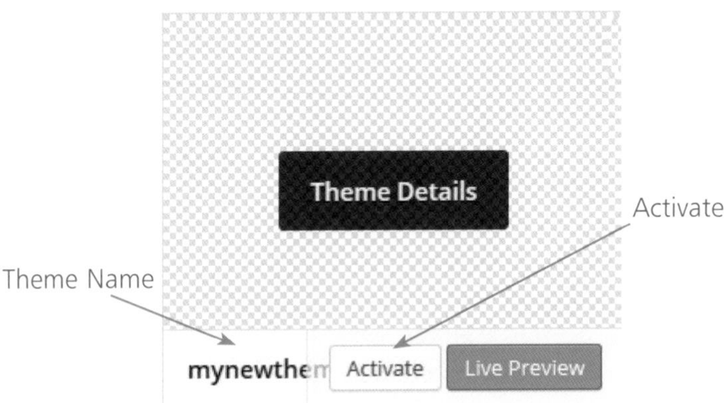

7. Now, click **Activate** and your theme should now be available on your live website

You can change back to another theme at any time by going back to **Appearance > Themes** from your Dashboard.

When activating a custom theme, there may come a time where the top WordPress bar might go missing. You can, however, access the WordPress Dashboard by going to **www.yourdomain.com/wp-admin/**

WordPress Backup

You should keep a backup of your whole WordPress website in case of a disaster or if you move web hosts. Earlier on in the book, we explained how to export posts and pages (see page 104). However, this is not the best method for backing up, because a WordPress website has multiple areas - things like stylesheets, plugins etc. You need to make sure the whole thing is backed up so that once your website is restored, it will be in the same state it was when you backed up.

File Backup

First of all you need to backup all your files. You can do this using the FTP program FileZilla, introduced on pages 163-165.

1. Open up FileZilla
2. Enter your FTP details

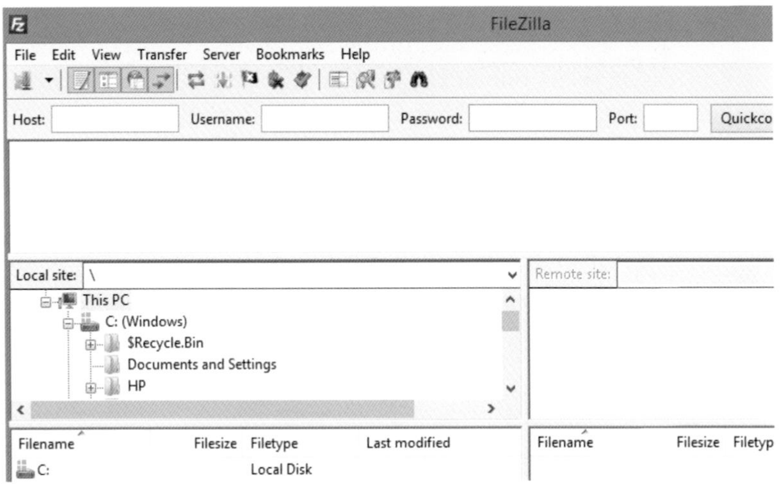

3. Make sure you create a directory on your computer where you want to store the backup

Create directory

Please enter the name of the directory which should be created:

Backup

OK Cancel

As well as keeping a backup on your computer, it may be a good idea to store your files on a backup disk or in the cloud.

...cont'd

4. Now, select that directory in the left window panel, ready to transfer the files across

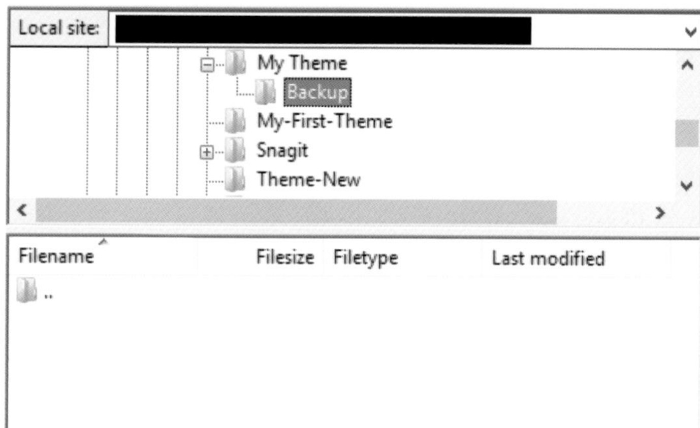

5. As you are logged in, and in the correct directory, you can now select all the files in the right panel. To make things easier, select one of the folders in the right panel and then press **Ctrl + A** on your keyboard so that all the files are selected

Filename	Filesize	Filetype	Last modified	Permiss
..				
cgi-bin		File folder	08/13/14 18:16:...	0755
wc-logs		File folder	02/02/15 20:44:...	0750
wp-admin		File folder	08/24/14 14:16:...	0755
wp-content		File folder	02/10/15 03:00:...	0755
wp-includes		File folder	11/14/14 09:19:...	0755
.ftpquota	15	FTPQUOT...	02/10/15 21:03:...	0600

6. Now, all you need to do is drag across the files from the right hand window, to the left hand window as shown in the screenshot on the next page. This copies the files to the location on your Desktop

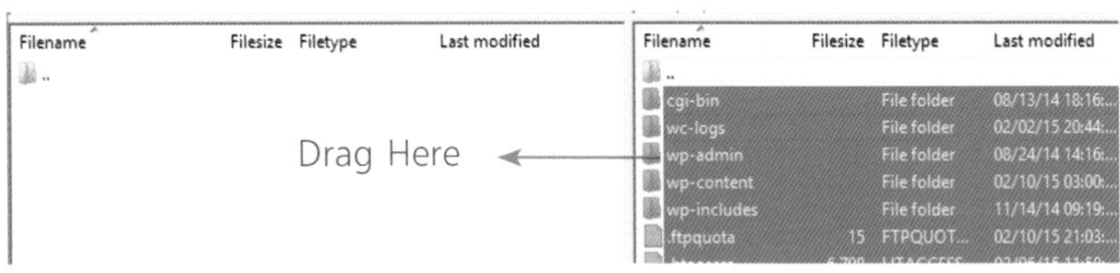

Make sure you have copied across every file, to avoid errors when restoring a backup.

Now you have copied all the files, you need to make a backup of the database. You can use phpMyAdmin which is located in your hosting control panel. We covered installing WordPress from the Control Panel in Chapter 1. Go back to this Control Panel to back up your website database.

Database Backup

1. Go to your hosting control panel and log in
2. You will need to scroll down until you find **phpMyAdmin**

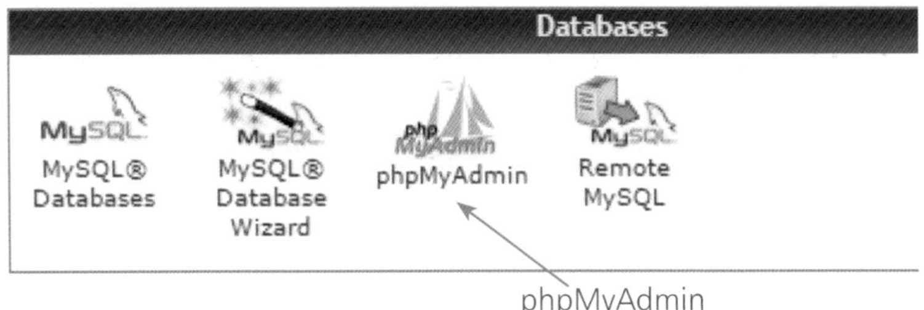

3. Select **Databases** along the top

4. You will be presented with a list of databases as shown on the next page. It is likely that you only have one database at this time; this is the WordPress database

...cont'd

You will need to click on the database (it will appear as a link under Databases)

5. You will be presented with a list of tables relating to WordPress. A lot of them will start with "**wp_**". For example, "**wp_users**". Ignore these and select "Export" along the top

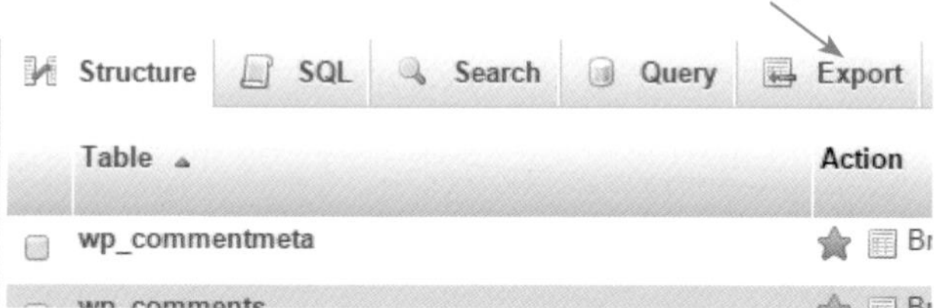

6. Select an export method and format. Select **Quick** under export method and for the format select **SQL**

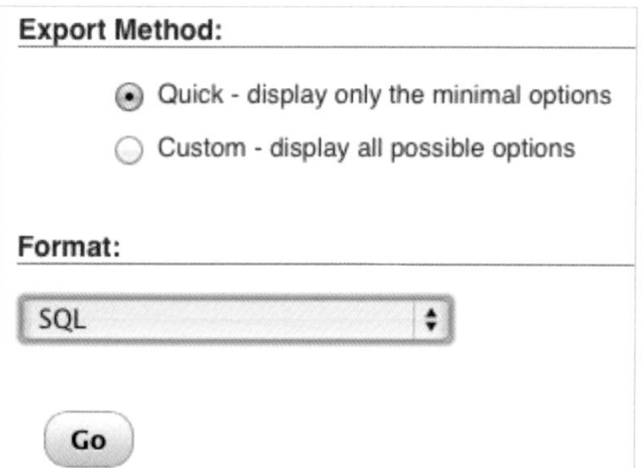

7. Finally, press the Go button. This will download the database locally to your computer

Make sure the database file is saved, along with your website files. You now have a complete backup of your website.

Responsive Design

There are more and more people using mobile phones and tablets to access the Internet these days. This makes it extremely important to make sure websites are responsive, so they appear and function properly across all devices.

These days, your website needs to cater for all kinds of devices, from smartphones to tablets. This means web developers need to look at customizing their sites for different resolutions.

Using a Responsive Theme

You could use a responsive theme, which would save a lot of time. ThemeForest do a good selection of responsive themes (**www.themeforest.net**), or you could search for "Responsive" when adding a new theme from the Wordpress Dashboard (see page 32). However, even if you have selected a great responsive theme, there might be times where you might want to move elements around – a bit like introducing CSS (see page 146).

Testing on Different Devices

You might very well own a selection of devices to test your website on, but this can be an expensive option. There are a number of browser tools you can use to test out your website's appearance across numerous devices.

One of the best ones to use is the **Web Developer Extension** by Chris Pederick. It is available for both Chrome and Firefox, and makes it easy to view your website using various resolutions.

Adding the Web Developer Extension

In this case we will use Firefox, but you can add it to Chrome if you wish.

1. Open up Firefox

2. Select **Tools > Add-ons** from the menu or **Ctrl + Shift + A**

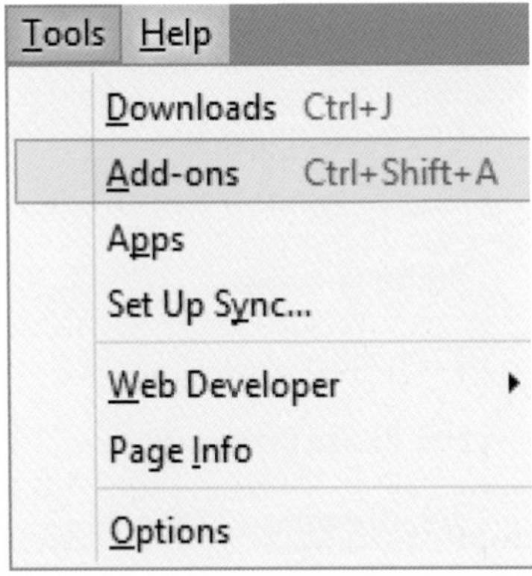

3. Select the **Web Developer** extension by chrispederick and install. You may be asked to restart the browser

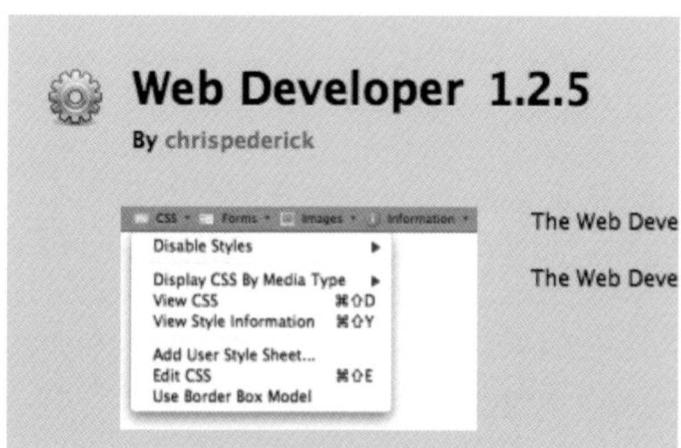

4. You should now have a bar added to your Firefox layout

Working with the Web Developer Extension

Now you have the extension installed, you are ready to view how your website looks across various resolutions.

1. Navigate to your WordPress website using the address bar
2. Select **Resize > View Responsive Layouts** from your extension bar

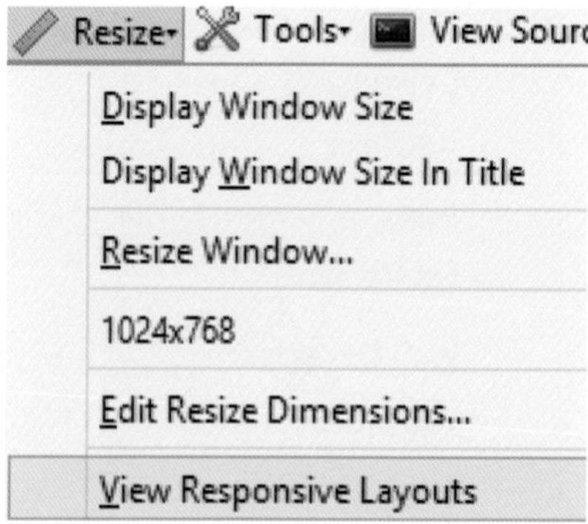

You should see that Firefox will bring up a number of viewpoints, displaying how your website will look using different devices.

There is nothing like testing your website on an actual device. If you have a mobile or tablet, be sure to test it out on the real thing.

▾ **Mobile landscape (480x320)**

MENU

TriEasy Triathlon Coaching

Professional Coaching for every Triathlete from Beginner to Elite

If you chose a responsive WordPress template when starting out development of your website, then most layouts should already look pretty good.

▾ **Small tablet landscape (800x600)**

PRICING TESTIMONIALS EVENTS BL

TriEasy Triathlon Coaching

Professional Coaching for every Triathlete from Beginner to Eli

...cont'd

Making Changes to a Responsive Template

You are now going to make changes to your mobile responsive layout. We will be using the element inspector (page 146) alongside the Firefox Web Developer Extension.

1. Select **Resize > View Responsive Layouts** from your extension bar in Firefox

Use the viewpoint at the top labeled **Mobile portrait (320x480)** to make changes to your mobile portrait mode

If you have a smartphone then you could view how your website displays on your device

2. Right click on one of the elements inside the mobile portrait viewpoint and click **Inspect Element**

3. You will notice the inspector appears at the bottom of the page, just like it did on page 146 when we introduced you to CSS. Make sure the correct element is selected. In this example we have right clicked on the main title in our inspector, which is **h1.** Yours might be different depending on your element

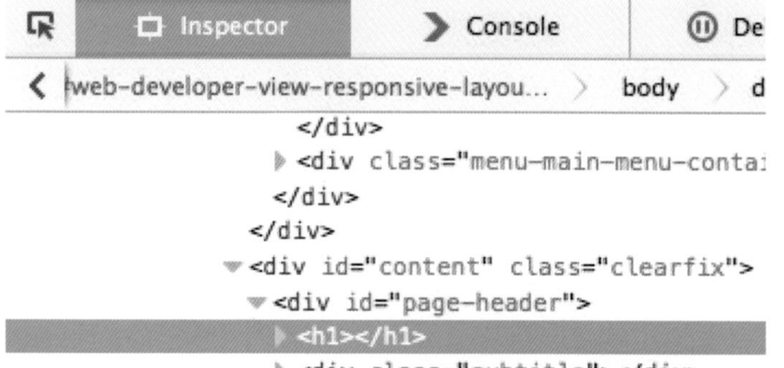

4. You should now notice on the right hand side, there is a specific piece of CSS for the h1 code for that screen size

```
  style.css:1555 @media…nd (max-width: 479px)
#page-header h1 {
     font-size: 28px;
     line-height: 40px;
     margin-bottom: 7px;
}
```

You should see something that looks like the following piece of code:

```
@media only screen and (max-width: 479px) {
        ELEMENT NAME {
               }
               }
```

This will set the element details for any screen size with a maximum width of up to 479 pixels. As shown on page 146, you can test how you want your element to look. This will only change the element for that particular screen size.

If you are using a responsive template from a third party website, remember that not all elements will have been modified for that particular screen size.

...cont'd

It is important to make sure in the Inspector that you can see the media only code. If that does not appear, then you will be changing the code for all resolutions.

```
style.css:1555 @media…nd (max-width: 479px)
```

It also displays the line of code in the stylesheet where the element detail is listed. In this case it is line 1555 of the style.css file.

5. You now need to open up your style.css file. You can do this by downloading it through FTP, or by going to **Appearance** > **Editor** and selecting your style.css file

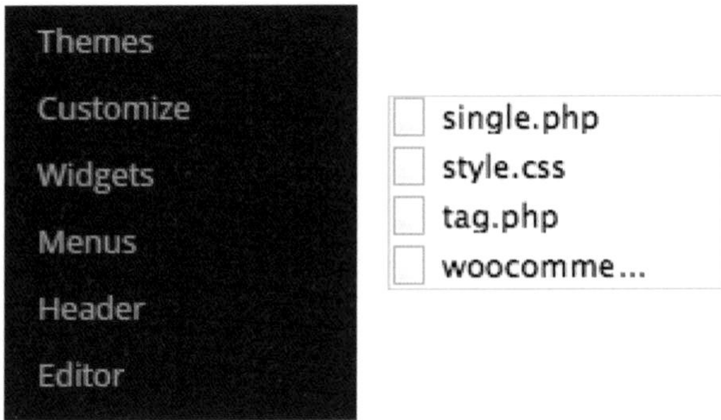

Using a code editor is a much better way to find pieces of code that have already been generated. Try to find an editor that displays the line number next to each line.

6. Find the element you need to change, but make sure it is under the correct screen size. You can do this by sticking to the line number that was displayed in your inspector. In this case it was line number 1555

```
#page-header h1 {
        font-size: 35px;
        line-height: 40px;
        margin-bottom: 7px;
}
```

7 After you have saved your changes, make sure you clear your browser cache. Sometimes during development you will need to do this, as your website might not update right away. You can do this in Firefox by selecting **History > Clear Recent History** from the main toolbar

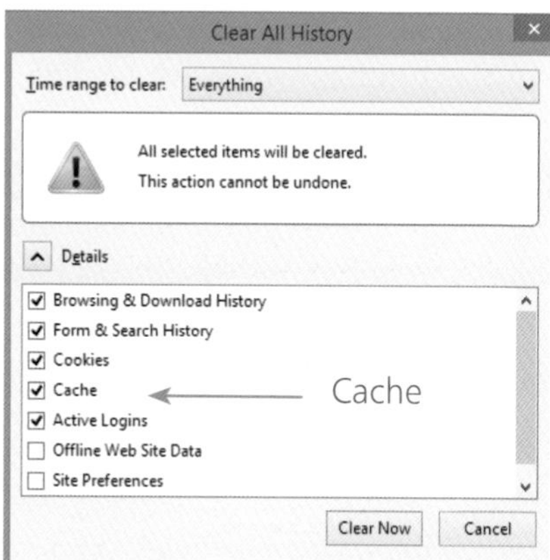

8 Now you will need to boot up your website again in Firefox using the responsive mode layout that was introduced on page 179. You can also boot up your WordPress website on your mobile device

Adding Responsive Layouts to the Stylesheet

If you are building your WordPress template from scratch, or you are using a non-responsive template, then there is a good chance you will not have the responsive layouts set up in your stylesheet. You will need to go into your style.css file to set these up manually.

The first thing you need to do is familiarize yourself with the layouts that you will need. A good way to do this is to use the widths provided in the Firefox responsive layouts.

▾ Mobile portrait (320x480)

The above example is 320x480. This means the width is 320 and the height is 480. Each individual layout will be different. For example, mobile landscape will be 480x320.

Open up your style.css file and go right to the bottom. The stylesheet is read from top to bottom, so the resolutions will need to go from highest to lowest, so the mobile resolutions will be the last ones to go on the sheet.

```
@media only screen and (max-width: 767px) {

Enter element styles here

}


@media only screen and (max-width: 480px) {

Enter element styles here

}
```

It is best to set up each media screen first, and then preview your changes using the Firefox Responsive Layouts, so you can get a good idea of your changes.

Index

A

B

C

D

E

F

G

H

I

L

M

N

O

P

R

S

T

U

V

W

Y

Notes